MASTERING
CONFLICT &
CONTROVERSY

MASTERING
CONFLICT &
CONTROVERSY

Edward G. Dobson
Speed B. Leas
Marshall Shelley

THOMAS NELSON
Since 1798

MASTERING CONFLICT AND CONTROVERSY
© 1992 by Christianity Today, Inc.
Published by Multnomah Press
10209 SE Division Street
Portland, Oregon 97266

Multnomah Press is a ministry of
Multnomah School of the Bible
8435 NE Glisan Street
Portland, Oregon 97220

Printed in the United States of America.

Library of Congress Cataloging-in-Publication Data

Davis, Ron Lee.
    Mastering conflict and controversy / Ron Lee Davis, Edward
G. Dobson, Speed Leas.
       p. cm. — (Mastering ministry)
    ISBN: 978-1-4185-3235-2
      1. Church controversies. I. Dobson, Edward G. II. Leas, Speed,
1937- . III. Title. IV. Series.
BV652.9.D38 1992
250—dc20   91-38337
                                           CIP

92 93 94 95 96 97 98 99 00 01 - 10 9 8 7 6 5 4 3 2 1

Contents

Introduction

It was the first sign of conflict in my new congregation: Jane, an elderly member of the choir, pulled me aside as I left worship and walked toward our fellowship hall for coffee.

"Mark, I'd be careful if I were you," she said in hushed tones. "Some people didn't like what you said about not clapping for the choir."

I had mentioned that subject during "Worship Remarks," a section of our service where I taught briefly about the meaning of worship. Especially after rousing numbers, our congregation had been in the habit of breaking out in applause. As a young minister, who *knew* what were and were not appropriate expressions of praise to the Almighty, I was not happy.

So in my remarks, I tactfully reminded people of the traditional Presbyterian understanding of the choir's purpose: the choir wasn't singing *to* the congregation, but *for* it *to* God. I concluded on the diplomatic "So that's why some people object to clapping after a special musical number — it seems to distract momentarily from God."

Well, I walked nervously into coffee fellowship, eyes darting, body braced to see who would pounce on me first. However, my newly formed enemies were gracious that morning, saving their assault about my "self-righteous" and "insensitive" comments until a committee meeting later in the month!

That's one of the things that never ceases to amaze me about church conflict — it often hinges on the seemingly inconsequential: whether we clap in worship, who will play Mary in the Christmas play, whether worship begins at 9:00 or 9:30, that the youth group forgot to put away two frying pans in the kitchen.

Other aspects of conflict have also puzzled me: How do I know if the fight over clapping, for instance, is really over theology, politics, or personalities? And when should I as pastor intervene in conflict between two members? How do I preach about controversy without making things worse?

These and other mysteries of church conflict, about which many pastors struggle, are unraveled in this volume of Mastering Ministry. We have brought together three authors who know conflict and how to deal with it.

Edward Dobson

Ed Dobson's background would suggest that he is first and foremost a fighter.

He was born and reared in Northern Ireland, a land not known for having mastered conflict.

He also spent a few years working as vice-president of Liberty University, in Lynchburg, Virginia, under Jerry Falwell, a man who has enjoyed his share of controversy.

He's appeared on countless television and radio shows, often in hostile settings, where he's been asked (to put it mildly) to give reasons for the hope within him.

But although Ed is familiar with conflict and controversy, he's not first and foremost a fighter.

First, he's a pastor, right now at Calvary Church in Grand Rapids, Michigan. Second, he's an evangelist, seeking actively to reach people for Christ.

And with those priorities, he puts conflict, especially over issues, into perspective:

"In the nineties, we need to demonstrate our genuine concern for issues, but we can't become associated with a political party or one-issue agenda," he said recently. "If I'm to reach Grand Rapids, that means reaching the National Organization for Women; it means reaching Planned Parenthood; it means reaching Democrats and Republicans, Hispanics and blacks, religious and non-religious. I have to figure out a way to be true to my values without unnecessarily wiping out my credibility with a segment of the community."

So Ed has learned to speak clearly and forcibly when the Bible calls him to and to talk diplomatically and graciously otherwise. He's been in the fray more than once in his ministry, but those experiences have taught him how to handle himself so that the message and love of Christ get out in spite of the conflict.

In addition to fulfilling his pastoral and administrative duties through the years, Ed has found time to write with Jerry Falwell and others *The Fundamentalist Phenomenon* (Revell), and with Ed Hindson, *The Seduction of Power* (Revell), as well as a few volumes of his own.

In this book, Ed, like the others, has contributed four chapters, the most gripping of which is "Restoring a Fallen Colleague," the story of the fall and restoration of Truman Dollar. It's an extremely personal story, and Ed worked very closely with Truman in preparing it. We include it because it is a unique type of controversy that a few pastors face.

Speed Leas

The grandfather of Speed Leas was named for Joshua Speed, a farmer and acquaintance of Abraham Lincoln. He and Lincoln corresponded regularly, in fact, and they argued heatedly over the divisive issue of their day: slavery. Despite their deep differences, their letters display civility and a genuine respect for each other.

That ability to disagree agreeably has apparently become a trait of the Leas family, if Speed is any indication. Although, to hear him tell it, he's not all that comfortable with conflict:

"I've always struggled with conflict in my life. Conflict has been hard for me. I haven't understood it, and I haven't understood myself when I've been in conflict. My work is partly a quest to understand what happens to me when I get in a conflict, so I can do better."

That quest has taken him to Yale Divinity School, where he earned M.Div. and S.T.M. degrees and then to United Emmanuel Church of Christ in Watts, in Southern California (where, during his tenure, the Watts riots broke out).

He also spent some time with Saul Alinsky, learning about organizing communities, but he found that Alinsky's *Rules for Radicals* didn't work for the church.

Within a few years the activist became a peacemaker. His study of organizational change and management led to the book *Church Fights* (Westminster, written with Paul Kittlaus), and later, to *Leadership and Conflict* (Abingdon). Soon he was consulting churches and lecturing at seminaries. In 1977 he joined the Alban Institute, through which he is constantly on the run, helping churches (and himself!) learn how to deal with the tensions they face.

Marshall Shelley

Marshall Shelley is an editor, who, among other things, spends his days reviewing manuscripts, fixing stray punctuation, and determining where to lengthen or shorten articles — hardly the atmosphere in which to know the rage of church controversies.

Then again, Marshall has for nine years been editing a unique magazine: LEADERSHIP, a practical journal for church leaders. So he has put his keen eye to hundreds of articles about church life, and to prepare the journal year after year, he's had extended conversations with thousands of pastors. In short, few people in America have as much contact with as many pastors from as many situations as does Marshall.

Marshall knows churches, and so he knows church conflict. In addition to a couple of years in the pastorate and his ongoing involvement in his church, he can view church conflict as a *journalist* outsider — one who knows how to analyze a situation and get to the heart of issues.

That's one reason that among pastors and church leaders his *Well-Intentioned Dragons: Ministering to Problem People in the Church* (Word) is among the most well-known books on church conflict.

In this volume, Marshall offers one chapter of his own and introduces three from other authors whose insights have been beneficial to pastors. In addition to being editor of LEADERSHIP, he is an editorial vice-president of Christianity Today, Inc.

One well-known preacher of the last century said, "Shut out suffering, and you see only one side of this strange and fearful thing, the life of man. Brightness and happiness and rest — that is not life. It is only one side of life. Christ saw both sides."

In this volume, we offer you the other side of church life. It's not pleasant, but it is real. Nor is it easy to work through, but it is redeemable, as our authors will show.

— *Mark Galli*
associate editor, LEADERSHIP
Carol Stream, Illinois

Part 1
The Upside of Conflict

Politicians are satisfied with 51 percent of the constituency behind them. Pastors, however, feel the pain when even one critic in a hundred raises his voice.

— Marshall Shelley

CHAPTER ONE

David and Solomon: Two Sides of Conflict

Conflict in the church is unavoidable. It's been that way from the beginning. The church began with a remarkable blend of close community and simmering conflict.

The Book of Acts describes a peaceful atmosphere: "All the believers were together and had everything in common. . . . Every day they continued to meet together in the temple courts. They broke bread in their homes and ate together with glad and sincere hearts, praising God and enjoying the favor of all the people. And the Lord added to their number daily those who were being saved" (Acts 2:44–47).

Only a couple of pages later, however, the situation has changed. Not only is the church threatened by outside enemies, but the extraordinary unity within was apparently short-lived.

Complaints arose about the way the church was caring for widows. Later, the church was divided over lifestyle expectations for new converts. Still later, Paul and Barnabas sharply disagreed over a staffing decision, and they parted ways.

Procedures, prerequisites, personnel — all areas that continue to challenge church unity today.

Pastors may feel the effect of conflict in the church more than most. One reason is that relationships are the professional priority of pastors. They know their effectiveness in the church is often judged by how well people work together. A second reason is that pastors tend to be "people persons," relationally oriented. Getting along with people is important to them. And when relationships are strained, pastors often feel like failures.

Politicians are satisfied with 51 percent of the constituency behind them. Pastors, however, feel the pain when even one critic in a hundred raises his voice.

As editor of a journal for pastors, I've often sat with ministers who were discouraged by a church in conflict. They didn't know how to respond; they felt that they were somehow to blame for the very existence of conflict. Perhaps that's why the following story is so apt for pastors facing the trauma of a tussle.

When I first sat with Bob Moeller and heard his story, it resonated deep within me. He pastored two churches, and saw two completely different responses to his leadership. His story, and his biblical parallels, help clear our focus on conflict in the church.

Bob Moeller is now director of communications and assistant to the president of Trinity Evangelical Divinity School in Deerfield, Illinois. But his pastoral experience bleeds through his account.

He gives a couple of biblical models for leading God's people amid tension. His story shows that situations may be long-standing and bigger than any one individual. He also demonstrates that pastors may not be responsible for the difficulty, but they can act responsibly within the situation.

In short, his story helps put conflict in perspective.

* * *

My two pastorates couldn't have been more different. Two Sunday afternoons, less than three years apart, typify the contrasts.

The most recent afternoon began with an awkward lunch. The atmosphere reminded me of the meal following a funeral — people smile, comment on the food, but inwardly their hearts are broken. I knew mine was.

Joining us at the table was our district superintendent and an elder from a sister church in town. They had come at the request of our elder board to spend the afternoon listening privately to the complaints and accusations of individuals in our congregation.

What had begun sixteen months earlier as minor skirmishes was now a full-blown schism. The surface tension was over issues as petty as my decision to rearrange the office furniture. We also heard veiled complaints about the practice of certain spiritual gifts. But as I saw it, the real conflict was the issue of control — a small group in the church had served notice that *they* were in charge, not the board or the pastor.

I hoped that with the help of these experienced men from outside, we could confront the issues directly and resolve the conflict. But despite the encouraging words from the district superintendent, a long-time friend, I knew the truth: more than likely, my days of ministry there were ending. Regardless of who emerged victorious from the confrontation, the long conflict had taken its toll. There had been too many hurts, too many rumors, too many innuendoes and feelings of betrayal.

As with most church battles, the combatants were relatively few in number. I was reminded of a tactical lesson from military history: guerrilla forces need be only one-tenth the size of a conventional army to keep it hopelessly enmeshed in a no-win situation.

My wife and I were exhausted from the guerrilla warfare. We had nothing left to give. As I sat at the lunch table, waiting for the day's events to unfold, I recalled another, much different, more pleasant Sunday afternoon.

This other afternoon was farewell day at my previous pastorate. We were finishing five years of difficult but fulfilling ministry in the inner city. A group of people who had once been ready to disband and give their building to a parachurch organization were now alive and aggressive in their purpose and mission.

The church had grown. It was feeding street people and attracting Native Americans to worship services. It distributed hundreds of pounds of clothes to the destitute. At times, so much food for the poor was donated from supporting churches that we had to stack it in the front pews of the sanctuary. The shewbread was once again in the temple feeding the hungry.

My wife and I were overwhelmed with the love we received in that small urban church. One cold, winter day, a 94-year-old woman from the congregation walked to our home with her Norwegian stew because she'd heard I was ill.

The Sunday afternoon we left, I held back tears as the church chairman and his wife cried while saying good-bye. It had been a sweet experience, working together to build God's house in that place.

Two Different Roles

As I look back over these two experiences, a metaphor from the Old Testament helps me make sense of the two polar opposite pastorates: the life and destiny of David compared with that of Solomon.

David dreamed of building a temple for the Lord in Jerusalem. But he was prevented from doing so. God explained that it was not for him to be the architect and builder. David had been a warrior; he had shed too much blood. It would be his son Solomon who would construct the sanctuary and witness the glory of the Lord descend upon it.

Solomon reigned during a time of nearly unbroken peace in the land. He watched as his land blossomed with prosperity undreamed of by his ancestors. He watched as the temple grew and took form, and he led in the exhilarating experience of dedicating the building, when God himself appeared, to enter the Holy of Holies. His string of successes were untarnished for years on end.

Reflecting on my experiences, and those of other pastors, I've noticed that each of us may find ourselves following the path of David or Solomon or both during our ministries. We may play the role of a warrior in one setting and that of a temple builder in another. Perhaps both are in the will of God. Certainly each has inherent in them certain advantages and risks.

What Happens to a David

Some pastors find themselves in the role of a David; they're perceived as warriors who challenge well-established and powerful forces. Such an individual is willing to endure conflict in order to address moral and spiritual issues that are vital to the well-being of the body, thereby clearing the way for the church's future growth and ministry.

Few if any Davids remain in such a setting long enough to witness the grandeur of the completed temple. The cost of battle often is so high they become a casualty themselves, even if their cause is victorious.

These individuals are not contentious personalities who thrive on conflict, obsessive in their need to control others, who see their lives as a martyr's lot. These are not the traits of a David. A true David finds such conflict in the church sad, painful, and regrettable but at times necessary.

What happens to a David? Let me suggest some advantages, dubious as they might seem at first, that result from serving as a David.

• *You lay the groundwork for future church growth and spiritual prosperity.* One maxim of church history is that the blood of the martyrs is the seed of the church (Tertullian). In less dramatic terms, that means the sacrifice and pain borne in guiding a church to spiritual healthiness will someday be rewarded.

I once asked a friend why he was leaving a prominent Christian organization in my city. His reply: "Once you tell the truth, it's often impossible to stay." To a certain extent that can be true in a pastorate: truth-telling can make this awkward.

Early in my ministry I had to face a situation that existed in a women's Bible study. Under the guise of prayer requests, some women were telling stories about the failings of their husbands (or husbands of their friends). Not only was there potential for embarrassing individuals, relationships and careers could have been severely damaged. Though several women felt uncomfortable and vowed never to return to such a study, the practice went on for several years.

When I asked some of the leaders to exercise more discretion, they felt I was intruding on *their* ministry. It proved for me an unpardonable sin. From that day on, I was in trouble.

Yet, the strife that ensued eventually led to new leadership, who fostered a much healthier atmosphere and even opened the way for new women, particularly non-Christians, to be welcome in the group.

● *You learn that God is more concerned with what happens in you rather than to you.* In short, you attend the graduate school of character. As Chuck Swindoll says of suffering, "The tuition is free. It only costs you your life."

As I became more bewildered over why I was in such hard circumstances, I began to believe that God was in all this in some way I couldn't fully understand.

Interestingly, the Psalms became more practical and essential to my life than ever. And I learned what David learned: God is in control regardless of what people may do. I came not to hate criticism but to see it as an opportunity for God to examine my life and test my character. Was I able to respond gently, firmly, in an honorable way?

Though painful, I sensed a firmer foundation being laid in my faith.

● *You develop close and meaningful relationships with key church leaders.* There is no racism in foxholes. Likewise, the barrier between pastor and laity diminishes as you weather intense storms together. I came to love as brothers those who stood with me on the elder board. At great personal cost, they took action to discipline certain members of the congregation. Having been through some difficult hours together, we were a group who had become a team, even friends.

One of our elders, who had a history of heart problems, suffered a form of cardiac arrest while on the phone one night. After a leave of absence, to have a pacemaker inserted, he returned to the church more committed than ever to deal with the problems.

Such commitment is not found among "sunshine soldiers," as Thomas Payne called them. Neither is deep camaraderie.

But besides the advantages, there are also some definite risks to serving as a David.

● *You are misunderstood by those who have an inadequate theology of conflict.* Some people see all conflict as sin. Their conclusion: you must be in sin (or at least an incompetent pastor) or there would not be this trouble. In their minds, the only spiritual church is one that's free of conflict. While a conflict-free environment is everyone's goal, it is often only arrived at by working through significant and difficult issues.

During one congregational meeting, one person pointed at me and said, "The trouble started with you!"

While that may or may not be true, it doesn't always mean that trouble is unnecessary or unredemptive. I often think about the conflict in the ministries of the patriarchs, the prophets, Jesus, and the apostles. As they challenged wrong behavior or attitudes, they were perceived as the problem. As a result, some were sawn in two. At times, I've had a good idea what that must feel like.

● *Once cast as a warrior, it's almost impossible to change people's perception.* It's similar to the Leonard Nimoy syndrome. Nimoy was the actor who played Mr. Spock in the television series, *Star Trek*. His distinctive character became so well-known that no matter the roles Nimoy played in later years, no one could imagine him as anyone but Mr. Spock.

Once a pastor is identified as a warrior, that reputation is extremely hard to shake. I spent hours with individuals in counseling, visitation, and personal discipleship. I worked to keep a balanced pastoral ministry. Yet to those who wanted to believe it, I was simply obstinate, the one they said "can't get along with So-and-so."

Some of my critics were outspoken. One Sunday morning after church, I met a real estate company president who had visited our church. Thanking me for the morning message, he confessed he had come just to meet the man his secretary could not say anything nice about!

● *After prolonged conflict, you tend to lose perspective.* While you try to focus on issues and not personalities, the longer the battle, the more they change places.

After decades of bloody feuding, the Hatfields and the McCoys, it is said, couldn't remember what their initial argument was about. But that didn't matter any longer. The issue had become people, whether one was a Hatfield or a McCoy. So it goes in churches, and warriors can easily forget that they should battle issues not people.

In such moments the words of Jesus to love enemies and to be kind to the spiteful take on new significance. I knew I was making progress when I could honestly tell the husband of a woman who had caused me great suffering that I loved them both.

But many are the temptations to cover our buried anger with self-deceptions such as, "I don't hate them; I have only righteous indignation."

What Happens to a Solomon

Now let's consider what's involved in being a Solomon, first examining some advantages.

● *You receive affirmation and support from the congregation.* Unlike a David, who is often controversial and misunderstood, a Solomon is liked by nearly everyone. After all, the visible signs of growth and prosperity are evident, and it's easy to attribute at least some of that success to the pastor.

You don't leave such a church with many enemies, and even those who disagreed with you begrudgingly admit you helped the church. Given a little time, your accomplishments tend to grow in the retelling.

I've never enjoyed a larger-than-life reputation, but in that small urban church, people remembered fewer of my mistakes and more of my successes. During the height of the crisis in my second church, my wife and I took a summer vacation that included a Sunday morning stop at my previous parish. I was given the opportunity to speak, so I briefly updated them on my family and thanked them for their ministry to my family while we were with them. When I finished, the congregation broke into applause. Such affirmation seemed almost schizophrenic given the problems I was facing in my current pastorate, but it was deeply appreciated.

• *You observe the glory of God descend upon your church.* One of the great rewards of ministry is seeing the hand of God touch our efforts. Apart from our merit, God regularly chooses to do things beautiful if not miraculous in our ministries. Solomon's virtue was not the reason the glory of God descended on the temple at the day of dedication, yet Solomon was privileged to observe it and participate in that supernatural event.

In a similar way, I watched God work in our little church. We opened our church to the community for the first time on Thanksgiving. I had been there about three months, and though we had only seventy-five regular attenders, we ran an ad in the city newspaper, inviting people to come for a free turkey dinner with all the trimmings. The board members were nervous. What if there were problems? What if no one came? What if everyone came?

At sunset, as we opened the doors, I watched a stream of humanity pass through our doors and down to the basement — white, black, Hispanic, and Native American. Several of our ushers stood grimly with their arms crossed, ready for trouble. But none ensued, and by evening's end we had fed 250 men, women, and children from the community. Our joy and celebration were evident: after cleanup, our 63-year-old church chairman was seen skipping across the empty room.

I cannot say I saw the glory of God descend in the same way that Solomon did, but I knew I was in the presence of the Almighty that evening. It was the beginning of good things to come.

• *Your church is attractive to visitors.* Within five minutes of arriving, visitors can read the atmosphere of a church. Warmth, acceptance, and joy seem to exude even from the narthex of some buildings. On the other hand, as a visitor myself I've entered churches and immediately felt a stale, death-like pall that seems to linger in the air. Tension or routine seem the order of the day.

With all these heady benefits, it's easy to become oblivious to the risks of being a Solomon. But as many of us have learned, success can be far more treacherous to our spiritual well-being than failure. Consider some of the following not-so-obvious pitfalls of leading a united and prosperous parish.

● *You are tempted to believe that your leadership alone is responsible for the great things that have happened.* Watching programs expand and the budget rise is fun. It's also dangerous, particularly if, as I was, you are young and in your first pastorate. I was naive enough to believe I was largely responsible for this success, and the devil helped nurse that illusion at every opportunity.

It takes a more seasoned and less presumptuous pastor to realize that if you are experiencing a time of relative peace and prosperity, others have probably paid an anonymous but enormous price to help pull that off. Somewhere on your property there ought to be a monument to The Unknown Pastor: that brave and selfless soul who gave some of his or her best years to lay the groundwork for the good things that are now happening.

Presumption is perhaps pride in its purest form. Herod welcomed the praise of the people when they proclaimed he was a god. Few of us are that arrogant, but still we secretly delight in overhearing conversations in which another credits the church's growth to our arrival. It's as deceptive as the lie that says all the trouble began when we arrived. The truth lies somewhere between: we inherit more than we create as pastors, whether for good or ill.

Looking back at my inner city experience, I can think of a long line of pastors who invested their lives in that place, and the one who served immediately before me perhaps deserves more praise than the rest. He stayed only two years. But in that time he argued that business as usual was no longer possible. By the time I came, the people were ready to listen. Though few realize it, I owe that young pastor and his wife most of my subsequent success.

• *You are tempted to embrace neo-prosperity theology.* In short, you are led to believe that God's will for every pastor is to experience unbroken success and prosperity. To paraphrase Garrison Keillor, all the programs are good looking, and all the attendance figures above average. How wrong, perhaps even diabolical.

The writer of Hebrews tells us that God used many individuals in the past to accomplish feats of wonder. They conquered kingdoms, administered justice, gave the dead back to the living. But that's not where the chapter ends.

It concludes by talking about a second group, a group who were too good for this world. They were persecuted; they went about in animal skins; they even lived in holes in the ground. But from God's perspective, they are greater heroes than the first group.

How many of us think of the true heroes of the church as men and women who remain faithful while struggling in some lonely and forgotten town, selfish and angry critics constantly sniping at them. How can such sorrow and hurt be part of God's will? Doesn't he want us to live on an ecclesiastical roll? We'd all answer no, but at times, especially when the church was doing well, I'd tend to forget that.

During my second pastorate, it hurt to go to denominational gatherings, where others would boast of building programs and staff additions while I watched people leave my church because of conflict. I realized how smug I must have appeared the years figures were in my favor.

• *You are tempted to become hardened to others' pain.* According to the Arabic proverb, "All sunshine makes a desert." That is also true in living the life of a Solomon. It's easy to become, little by little, less sensitive to people in pain.

During my heyday, I enjoyed being around people I considered winners. I had little time for the individual who seemed headed nowhere. I believed I was on a life-track that would curve upward. If colleagues were in trouble, it was their fault.

Granted, my pastoral success was meager, but at the time it appeared significant to me, as well as to my colleagues who were struggling to survive in their churches. But as they reached out for help from me, I didn't listen. I'm afraid that on the road to Jericho I walked past many a wounded pastor and kept going.

When the tables were turned, though, I saw how shallow I had become. I was sharing my hurts with a fellow pastor one day. He listened with feigned patience and then replied, "You know, I've never experienced anything like that. Everywhere I have gone I've had a wonderful experience. I can't remember anyone leaving my churches in anger."

At first I felt hurt, then rage, then finally sorrow. He was handicapped. His own relative ease had disabled him from helping me. From that time onward, I no longer cursed my problems but began to ask God what he wanted to do in my life through my pain. If possible, I would become a wounded healer.

Farewell to Arms

The day I, as David, drove out of my second church, only a few people stopped by to say good-bye. As my wife and I headed into the desert, I knew a chapter of my life had closed.

The people had been gracious: when I submitted my resignation, they voted to reject it. I will never cease to be amazed by the confidence these people had in me despite the fact that during my pastorate we had lost almost seventy-five people. They gave us time to reconsider our decision during a leave of absence, which coincided with the birth of our fourth child. Yet, as my wife and I considered the larger picture, it seemed time to go.

I had put down the sword. The war was over.

The day I, as Solomon, left my first church my wife and I clung to friends and cried. The temple doors were closing behind us.

Which experience do I value more, that of being a warrior or a temple builder?

Sigmund Freud once said something to the effect that someday, given enough time, those experiences of life that have been the most difficult will become to us the most precious of all. He was simply borrowing truth from Ecclesiastes which says God makes everything beautiful in his time.

I would gladly serve a thousand churches like my little inner city pastorate. But I would not trade all of them for my years in the desert.

Should a pastor be a warrior or temple builder?

Yes.

— *Robert Moeller*

Unless an organization encourages regular and thorough internal challenge to what it has been doing, it's unlikely to be able to keep up with the changing world.

— Speed Leas

CHAPTER TWO

Tension Isn't All Bad

One Presbyterian congregation of 150 members worried for years about its Sunday school program. Many members believed the church was losing potential members to two neighboring Presbyterian congregations (each of which had over a thousand members) because their church didn't have a large enough Sunday school program to attract and hold young couples with children. They would often apologize to newcomers about the insufficient Sunday school, promising they were working on enlarging it.

When the church called a new pastor, the members began

lobbying him about the need for a larger Sunday school program. So the pastor went to work.

He attended some church growth seminars, read literature, did some demographic studies, and finally came up with a plan. He presented it to the board.

"Within two miles of our church, in all directions," he said, "we have a high proportion of young couples with small children. If we target these families with appropriate advertisements, special programs, and more contemporary worship services, I'm sure we can significantly increase our worship and Sunday school attendance."

After explaining some of the details, the pastor invited discussion. The elders were uniformly disturbed.

"I don't feel very comfortable 'targeting' one group," said one. "It feels elitist."

"I like the fact that our little congregation spans the generations," said another in her early thirties. "I don't know that I would have gotten to know some of the older members and some young people had there been more people my age."

"Why do we have to compete with our sister churches anyway?" said another still. "If people want a huge program, let people go there. If they want a small, intimate fellowship, let them come to us."

And on it went, until the pastor's frustration became intolerable.

"Now wait a minute," he interrupted. "You've been complaining for years about low Sunday school attendance. I present you with a plan for dealing with the problem, and you say you like things the way they are."

There was silence.

"It seems to me we have a choice," the pastor continued. "Either we make some changes to bring in some younger couples, or we accept the fact that we are the small, intimate, Presbyterian congregation in the area. But if we choose the latter, we need to stop complaining about our small Sunday school program."

The elders opted for the latter, and the complaining about the Sunday school virtually ceased. In fact, they began to see some of its many advantages (lots of contact with teachers, for example, both in and out of the classroom), and began "selling" these to newcomers.

Without open conflict, though, this situation would not have worked out so well. Members would have harbored their frustration for years longer, or the pastor would have resented the board's rejection of his proposal. In either case, people would have remained angry, and nothing would have been done to solve the problem.

It's just one of many instances in which church conflict produces good.

The Benefits of Conflict

One of the major reasons businesses fail (or decline) is that they cannot readily adapt to their changing environments.

When an organization figures out what works, it's tempted, naturally, to hold on to that wisdom. The problem is that what worked once may not work now: the competition has produced a better product, or financing is more difficult to obtain, or buyers are no longer interested in the product, or whatever.

Unless an organization encourages regular and thorough internal challenge to what it has been doing, it's unlikely to keep up with the changing world. Richard Pascale, author of *Managing on the Edge: How the Smartest Companies Use Conflict to Stay Ahead* (Simon and Schuster, 1990), says:

"*The* essential activity for keeping our paradigm current is persistent questioning. I will use the term *inquiry*. Inquiry is the engine of vitality and self-renewal. . . . Contention fuels the 'engine of inquiry' and is a cheap and abundant fuel. Yet contention carries a stigma: managers are uncomfortable with it, and it is often misconstrued as a sign of organizational ill health. This need not be the case."

Likewise, conflict in the church is not a sign of ill health. It produces, in fact, a great deal of good.

I'm not talking about a level of conflict in which there is bitterness and deep resentment (although even this level of conflict can turn out for good). To me, whenever people disagree, even if they disagree gracefully, that's conflict. And conflict has a number of benefits, the more important of which are these:

● *Issues get explored fully.* The small Presbyterian congregation that worried about its Sunday school program needed to come to grips with its situation. It was a small congregation that was trying to compete with two sister churches, both with over a thousand members, each located not more than three miles away, in opposite directions.

The people who had joined the church had done so precisely because it wasn't a large church. They liked the informal and intimate atmosphere. But they continued to feel intimidated by their "successful" sister churches.

When the conflict came to a head in the board meeting, they were able to see clearly the issues that troubled them. They recognized, as a result, what they really wanted in a church, and started acting accordingly.

● *Better decisions are made.* Without some tension, church leaders will not likely be motivated to get complete information on a problem. That lack of motivation, though, can cause its own problems.

One large congregation I worked with bought an expensive computer system. Since they bought it from a member of the congregation, whose business was computers, they bought it at a good price. Because of the man's offer, they neither studied the computer system carefully nor looked at other systems.

However, the new computer could not handle the needs of their congregation. It could manage data bases well, but it couldn't do the complex word processing needed for bulletins, newsletters, and other church mailings, nor could it handle the church's financial accounting.

In order to remedy their problem, they had to buy an additional computer to do the accounting and word processing. That embarrassed the seller of the computer, the board, and the business manager. If people would have asked the tough questions at the beginning, risking the conflict that might have ensued, perhaps they could have saved themselves both money and embarrassment.

• *People are more committed to decisions.* Good church decisions are those in which most of the members are fully committed to the decisions. When a church board decides to build a new building, the people, not just the board, have to be interested in putting up money for the project. When a committee decides to offer a new Bible study at the church, the program is a success only when members are interested enough to actually participate.

Commitment to a decision is usually the result of (1) understanding the decision and (2) participation in the decision. If I believe that I've had something to do with the creation of an idea, I am more likely to help carry it out.

Paradoxically, the essence of helping with an idea can be to challenge it, adding to or subtracting from or altering significantly the proposal. Unless those hearing a proposal are able to ask questions (serious questions) and raise objections (sometimes serious objections) they are not likely to commit themselves to the decision finally made.

Fostering Healthy Conflict: Asking Questions

Someone brings a proposal up in a committee meeting, but no one criticizes it. Nobody is enthusiastic about the idea, but certainly no one is antagonistic either. Committee members say non-committal things like "I don't think it would hurt anything" and "That certainly is an interesting concept you've got there, John."

The potential for a disastrous decision is apparent. People aren't discussing issues, they're not exploring options, and they're not participating in the decision.

Assuming that the proposal calls for a significant change, and therefore should engender some healthy conflict, what might be happening here?

• *Members may think they know enough.* I once worked with a congregation that was unhappy with the organist/choir director they had hired. The references of the person had been mixed; he apparently had had serious conflicts in previous positions.

But the committee was attracted to the candidate: he was married and had two children; he was handsome and presented himself well. He gave the impression that he had been misunderstood in the past.

So they hired him without a great deal of discussion. They hadn't taken seriously the problems they knew about. They discussed and made a decision thinking they knew enough. Soon, however, they found he was causing staff problems at their church.

● *Members may think they know what others want.* Jerry Harvey, in his *Abilene Paradox*, tells about a family who takes a trip to Abilene, not because anyone wanted to, but because each thought the others wanted to. Everybody ended up unhappy.

In some churches, the pastor, against his better wishes, starts another morning Bible study because he thinks people want it, and people attend at first because they think the pastor wants them there. They all enter into the Bible study without realizing that no one wants to really be in this class.

But because of a mutual lack of interest, the pastor doesn't put in his best efforts at preparing, and people don't attend regularly. After a while the pastor resents people because they don't come, and the people who do come are frustrated because the pastor doesn't seem to care.

● *Members may be unaware of changing conditions.* George Barna talks about this phenomenon in his book, *The Frog in the Kettle*:

"Place a frog in boiling water, and it will jump out immediately because it can tell that it's in a hostile environment. But place a frog in a kettle of room-temperature water, and it will stay there, content with those surroundings. Slowly, very slowly, increase the temperature of the water. This time, the frog doesn't leap out but just stays there, unaware that the environment is changing. Continue to turn up the burner until the water is boiling. Our poor frog will be boiled, too — quite content, perhaps, but nevertheless dead."

Sometimes church people don't raise their voices to challenge what the church is doing or not doing because they simply don't realize how different the church or community has become.

● *Members may not see weaknesses of church traditions and myths.* In one church I worked with, the women's fellowship group insisted on meeting only on weekdays in the middle of the day. That's the time the group had met for decades, and it continued to attract the women who had attended for years. So no one objected.

But they did notice that younger women weren't attending. And they worried about that. But after much hand wringing, they decided that the younger generation simply wasn't as committed to the church as they were.

The women were anxious, but they experienced no conflict because no one had made the connection that the tradition of the women's group, which had worked well in another generation, was no longer a strength — in fact, it prevented younger women, most of whom worked during the day, from attending.

● *Members may lack standards by which to evaluate.* This is a problem especially when it comes to personnel issues. Congregations with no standards for their staff, their leaders, and their committees often don't recognize when things aren't going well — at least not until the problems become enormous.

These four reasons for lack of appropriate conflict can be dealt with simply. In the case of evaluation standards, it's a matter of helping the congregation decide what they want the staff to do and determining how to evaluate them.

In terms of the other three, it's a matter of helping people see that more is at stake than they think. And that means asking questions, even ones whose answers seem obvious.

My wife is one of those people who, when she takes a class, asks questions of the professor to clarify what he's saying. Sometimes she ends up asking questions to which the answers may seem obvious, but often after class, other students will come up and say to her, "Thanks for asking that question; I didn't know what he was saying either" or "I thought I knew what he was saying, but by your asking the question, it made things clearer."

As a consultant, I ask churches some of the questions they should be asking themselves. And because such questions usually reveal something significant, churches begin getting the idea, and they soon get in the habit of asking questions themselves, even about things that seem obvious.

Fostering Healthy Conflict: Overcoming Denial

Actually, I think Richard Pascale understates organizations' feelings about conflict. Especially in churches, conflict not only carries a stigma, it also scares people. It scares me, even though I'm convinced that conflict, in appropriate doses, can be of great value to a church.

This to me is the greater problem to overcome. Lack of information is one thing. Lack of courage to confront problems is another.

When I enter a church situation, I look for a number of signals — actually signs of denial — that tell me the congregation is afraid of dealing with conflict. Here are a few and how I respond to them.

● *What differences?* When I enter a congregation, I first gather information about the conflict that people have invited me to help with. At that point, they give me the straight story about the problems because they don't really believe they'll have to do anything about it — they think others in the church, those who are "wrong," will have to make changes.

When I finally tell people what I have learned and make recommendations about how they might proceed, suddenly they can't remember why they asked me to work there! Just when they should be getting serious about addressing the conflict, I often hear the words, "We don't really know why we invited you. It's really not that big of a deal." Strange but true.

I also see it when a pastor leaves a church under adverse circumstances. At that point, some people say, "Well, that conflict is over. We've gotten rid of that problem!" But they are simply denying the pain and frustration of those who feel lost without a pastor or the fact that conflict still exists between members.

Sometimes churches, in an effort to deny real differences, will put problems in a different light. That happens commonly in dysfunctional families: Uncle Bill abuses alcohol, and everyone knows it, but the family continues to say things like "Uncle Bill had to go to bed early because he isn't feeling well."

In churches I hear things like "The Pastor has other gifts besides administration" (but underneath lies a tremendous frustration about his poor planning) or "The treasurer is just fiscally conservative" (but underneath lies a deep resentment brewing about inadequate staff salaries).

● *Certain topics are off-limits.* Another sign of fear of conflict is a church's avoiding certain issues or topics.

For example, some congregations establish rules, written or not, that only the board can discuss controversial topics, like the church's stand on divorce and remarriage, or abortion, or local politics. People are strongly encouraged (from the pulpit or church newsletter or by general consent) not to discuss such issues with other church people — for the sake of unity, for the building up of the body, for many a good purpose.

I have seen congregational meetings deliberately structured so that nothing of interest or importance comes up. And when such matters do arise, they are efficiently tabled or referred to committee: "This is really not the time or place to discuss such a complex issue."

Such rules may have sound reasons supporting them, but when disagreements are always shunted off to small corners of the church's life, it tells me that an unhealthy fear of conflict infects the congregation.

● *Disgruntled people are encouraged to leave.* Over and over, I hear a similar speech in many churches: "If you don't like it here, there are plenty of other churches in town; consider going to one of them" or "Either get with the program or get out!"

Even when the speech is not spoken by a member of the congregation, an inner voice often tells people: "I shouldn't make waves here. If things don't go well for me, the best thing is to drop out."

● *A staff member's feelings are being protected.* I have worked with a number of congregations in which one problem has been the organist. Usually the person has been the church organist for many,

many years. But age has caught up with the person, and everybody is painfully aware of it: her playing is too slow, she misses her cues, and her performance is excruciatingly imprecise.

But does anybody do anything about it? No. Everyone assumes it isn't polite to give people such bad news; it would hurt their feelings terribly. So they let it go on, to the embarrassment of the congregation, pastor, visitors, leaders, and sometimes the organist herself.

One or more of these signs of denial are likely to surface just after a church has faced a serious conflict. Members often go into a type of depression, and they are nervous about "it" happening again. Church leaders seem to be extra vigilant to suppress any sign of challenge to the general sense of peace and order. People are especially wary of bringing up certain subjects.

It is difficult to deal with denial. Usually it takes someone from the outside to point out what's going on. Such a person might be a consultant, a denominational executive, a pastor from another congregation, or an interim minister. In addition, as with all conflict, it takes a leader skilled and trained in conflict management to deal fruitfully with denial and conflict.

A technique I use when I'm in a denying church is to interview people in small groups, building an atmosphere of trust, so that people will be honest with me. Then I present my findings to the whole congregation. Talking about conflict in public often breaks through the strong denial patterns, which usually make conflict more difficult than it needs to be.

If the denial centers around written or unwritten rules, I encourage people to break the rules! I invite members to talk about their concerns. I help them know what others in the congregation are struggling with. I design meetings so that people are encouraged to participate, and when they do, I make sure their ideas are taken seriously.

Encouraging Good Conflict

When healthy conflict is not present, it is often due to a lack of information or the presence of fear, among other things. But in the ongoing life of a congregation, low-level conflict can be encouraged in a number of simple ways:

● *Preach about low-level conflict.* I encourage pastors to mention in sermons that by articulating differences in committees and groups, congregations can grow and mature.

● *Praise disagreement.* When people disagree with you or others in the congregation, affirm them for raising their concerns. Let them know that differences are appreciated, and that, in the long run, such disagreement enhances the church's life.

● *Mix up committees.* Encourage chairpersons to put people with different perspectives on their committees. Then encourage them to allow those differences to emerge in discussion so that the committee can come to stronger decisions.

● *Put newcomers on leadership boards.* Newcomers see things differently than long-standing members. What old timers have taken for granted, they will question. What the board sees as satisfactory, they will wish was better. A newcomer's fresh perspective will likely generate conflict, although newcomers, reticent as they are, will need to be encouraged to speak out.

● *Set standards for the work of the church.* Once a year, have committees and boards look at what has happened in the church and ask "How did we do?" and "What can we do better?" If not the first year, certainly by the second and third, members will start getting the idea that disagreement and challenge is genuinely being sought.

● *Make clear the rules of healthy conflict.* Often congregations are worried that low-level conflict will escalate and become destructive. That fear and possibility can be alleviated if at least three rules of conflict are mentioned from time to time:

— No hitting!

— No personal attacks.

— No talking about people behind their backs.

In encouraging conflict, of course, the pastor has to be prepared to handle it appropriately. That takes training and practice. But it is not beyond the abilities of those who work with people day in and day out.

It Works

Saint Paul's, a church in a New York City suburb, had conducted a thorough, nationwide search and eventually called Dennis Roberts as their new pastor. The search committee had represented all voices in the church, including the trustees (the financial board) and the session (the administrative board), which had for a few years been in conflict. The committee, however, had done such a thorough and careful job, that in the end, the leadership of the church was unanimous about the selection.

Pastor Roberts had met with a sub-committee of the search committee (made up of three men, one of whom was an active trustee at that time) to discuss his salary, perquisites, housing, and moving costs. They easily came to an agreement, and a contract was drawn up.

As part of the negotiations, Pastor Roberts had asked if, instead of using the church's parsonage, he could purchase his own home. He had owned his home in the Midwest, from where he had come, and he knew he would make a tidy sum in capital gains when he sold it. He thought real estate a good, safe place to invest his money, and he liked owning his own home.

The sub-committee assured him this would be no problem. Another of the pastoral staff could live in the parsonage, or the church could rent it, or perhaps even sell it to Roberts, if he decided he liked the house. In any case, they suggested Roberts first move into the parsonage and live there while he and the church explored various alternatives for his housing. Pastor Roberts agreed with this plan, understanding that the details would be worked out later.

Roberts's first year at Saint Paul's was a smash hit. He hired a music director, who within six months increased the choir from fourteen to thirty. The church also called an associate who was an excellent pastor and administrator.

Roberts averaged seventy people in his Sunday Bible class, and members were astounded that he could speak knowledgeably about the Bible and Israel for forty-five minutes without a note before him. In addition, attendance was up at both of the services on Sunday, and a substantial number of new, young families joined the church. Most people gave the credit for all this to Pastor Roberts.

About nine months after he arrived, Roberts became increasingly concerned about his living arrangements. Soon he would owe $50,000 in capital gains taxes. He didn't want to take his one-time capital gains tax deferment because he felt he might need it more in the future.

Certainly he and his wife liked the parsonage: it was a beautiful home on the edge of a prestigious golf course; it was large enough to entertain church groups and close to the church; it had a beautiful study in which he enjoyed working. But he needed to buy a home.

So he started to bring up regularly with the trustees and the session the subject of his housing. This annoyed the trustees, most of whom were long-time members of the church. They told him, "Don't you have a perfectly adequate arrangement now? What would we do with the parsonage if you moved out? If you owned your own house, we'd have to pay you a housing allowance — we don't know if we can afford that."

But Roberts reminded them, "The search committee made a deal with me. I'll admit it was informal, but you did agree that I would be able to buy my own home when I moved to New York."

Reluctantly, the trustees set up a sub-committee to look into the situation and make a recommendation.

The sub-committee and pastor finally agreed that he would buy the parsonage, and they settled on a fair price. While the trustees were not all in favor of the sale, they voted eight to five to recommend to the congregation the sale of the parsonage to the pastor.

In the State of New York, though, the sale of any property must be approved by a two-thirds congregational vote. When the session announced a congregational meeting to vote on the sale, the trustees who voted against the sale talked with their friends about "Rev. Roberts's maneuvering" to get the parsonage. They weren't sure it was wise to sell the parsonage — they might need it down the road. And besides, said one trustee, "The way these people (meaning the session) spend money around here, the cash from this capital asset will be spent before you know it, and we won't have two nickels to rub together ten years from now when we're really going to need it."

At the congregational meeting, the chairwoman of the trustees spoke for the motion, but she was less than enthusiastic, though she said nothing clearly against it. Two trustees spoke against the motion. One of them, who had been on the search committee, said, "In fact, I don't remember any agreement to sell the parsonage to Rev. Roberts."

When the vote was finally taken, it lacked the necessary two-thirds majority by ten votes.

The session members, most of whom were younger members, were appalled. They spent their entire next meeting discussing the trustees' sabotaging of the new pastor.

One of the session members visited the home of the trustee who had been on the search committee. "You lied to the congregation!" he said. "If you can't support the leadership you helped call to the church, then you ought to leave!"

This confrontation so infuriated this trustee and others that a group began meeting to discuss the problems at the church. At their second meeting, they made a list of the difficulties now being faced by Saint Paul's. Among their charges, they said that the pastor was trying to stack the nominating committee and that he wanted to "get rid of" the trustees by restructuring the church boards.

When the session heard about these meetings, they decided to send session members to the trustees' meetings to monitor their discussions. The trustees tried to declare their meetings closed, but the session members present refused to leave.

Here were all the elements of formidable church conflict. Are we to conclude that this was "good" for the church? It was and it wasn't.

Clearly the tension was high, and the pain was real. But the church had been avoiding a number of issues over its history that were presenting themselves, in particular the tension between the session (representing newer members) and the trustees (representing older members). This issue, which had been brewing for years, was not worked through until a significant amount of tension arose.

The congregation dealt with this problem at several levels. First, with the help of an outside consultant, the trustees and session each agreed to send six representatives to a meeting in which the issue of the parsonage could be discussed openly and fairly. The representatives met for nine hours over two days, and the representatives became increasingly aware of the deeper concerns of each other. They were finally able to come to an agreement: the congregation would pay the pastor's capital gain taxes, and the congregation would retain the parsonage. The Robertses would continue to live in the parsonage and invest their money elsewhere.

Next, the church worked on the dissension between the newcomers and long-time members. The congregation had a meeting, which lasted all day Saturday, at which members were asked to assess how they had traditionally handled their differences. Then they drew up a list of guidelines and agreed to follow them when differences arose or people voiced concerns. Some of the guidelines were

1. *Conflict can be healthy and useful for our church. It is okay for people to differ with one another.*

2. *Resolutions for the sake of quick agreement are often worse than agreements that are carefully worked out over time.*

3. *Fair conflict management includes*

— *Dealing with one issue at a time,*

— *If more than one issue is presented, agreeing on the order in which the issues will be addressed,*

— *Exploring all the dimensions of the problem(s),*

— *Exploring several alternative solutions to the problem(s).*

4. *If any party is uncomfortable with the forum in which the conflict is raised, it is legitimate to request and discuss what the most appropriate forum might be.*

5. *Inappropriate behavior in conflict includes, but is not limited to*

— *Name calling,*

— *Mind reading (attributing evil motives to others),*

— *Inducing guilt ("Look how you've made me feel"),*

— *Rejecting, deprecating, or discrediting another person,*

— *Using information from confidential sources or indicating that such information exists.*

6. *Fair conflict always allows people who are charged with poor performance or inappropriate behavior*

— *to know who their accusers are,*

— *to learn what their accusers' concerns are,*

— *to respond to those who accuse.*

With these and other agreements in place, the congregation, especially the trustees and session, were able to work through a variety of conflicts. That, in turn, brought them closer together and allowed them, instead of getting mired in disagreements, to move forward.

And that's the point: conflict isn't all bad. When handled well, the seemingly bad situation can blossom into a greater good.

Part 2
Keeping Your Poise

How we respond to criticism reveals a lot about our calling and our composure.

— *Marshall Shelley*

CHAPTER THREE

Confidence Amid Criticism

I've always enjoyed the blend of lofty ideals and gritty realism of Jonathan Edwards, who once wrote:

"*Resolved: that all men should live for the glory of God. Resolved second: that whether others do or not, I will.*"

That resolve is rarely put to a greater test than when we are on the receiving end of pointed criticism.

Sometimes the criticism is subtle: "*I think you'd benefit from listening to this tape of one of my favorite radio preachers. He really gives you the meat of the Word.*"

Other times the criticism is sharp: "In your sermons, I don't appreciate the way you use (pick one) humor / Scripture / contemporary analogies / personal illustrations."

Still other times, it's scathing: "Ever since you've come here, you've been prostituting the gospel."

How we respond to such attacks reveals a lot about our calling and our composure.

John Cionca has, he admits, received both compliments and criticisms during his years of ministry. He served as minister of Christian education at Trinity Baptist Church in Mesa, Arizona, and later as senior pastor of Southwood Baptist Church in Woodbury, New Jersey. He is currently dean of students at Bethel Seminary in Arden Hills, Minnesota, and he frequently serves various churches as interim pastor.

It was shortly after making the switch from the pastorate to the academic world that he reflected on the "pastoral paranoia" he experienced with critics.

As someone once pointed out, the qualifications of a pastor are these: the mind of a scholar, the heart of a child, and the hide of a rhinoceros.

* * *

My ministry in Woodbury, New Jersey, began on a beautiful autumn day in 1979. With a successful eight-year ministry behind me and a strong conviction that the Lord was leading me, I optimistically began this new pastorate.

It didn't take long to immerse myself in the weekly details of study, administration, visitation, and counseling. I particularly enjoyed guiding the congregation in worship and the study of Scripture.

I had been preaching regularly for several years prior to this new position, but rarely, if ever, had I given much thought to how I was doing. My preaching task was simply to present the Word of God to the people of God. Oh, there were times for evaluation, but never had I become deeply introspective.

I began preaching in my new church with that same lack of self-consciousness.

Toward the end of my first year, however, I began reflecting more on myself as the communicator than on the message being communicated. The freedom of concentration on the Word was slipping. Increasingly my thoughts were *What are these people thinking about me?* rather than *What are they thinking about the biblical text?* I was becoming paranoid in my preaching.

The problem began with a number of "little foxes" that started to create self-doubt. My custom was to provide study outlines to accompany each text, and I began hearing some indirect comments like "Look at all the paperwork we have around here" and "It seems as if we're back in school again." The statements were not frequent, but they popped up enough to make me question the value of the outlines.

Another challenge to my preaching style, and more deeply, to me personally, was a comment by two individuals regarding my humor. One man told me that he'd heard a powerful sermon the previous day, and he added, the speaker had not shared one humorous incident in the entire message.

Now, I'm a smart enough boy to figure out this was not just a nice sermon report. Bob was telling me what he expected from the pulpit. Were there others who felt that way? Again, doubts were raised.

Then another fox began troubling my mental garden. Occasionally for illustrative purposes, I would mention an individual in the congregation. For example, if I were describing Palestine, I might say that the Sea of Galilee was located by Bill, and further down the Jordan River the Dead Sea would be located near Ed.

After one service, one man, Jerry, mentioned to me that although he was unlearned, he knew you should not mention a person's name in a speech. He said that names made him focus on the person named. In fact, on that particular Sunday, he spent the whole service reflecting on the lifestyle of the person I'd named in the service. He said that aspect of my preaching bothered him.

I appreciated Jerry taking the time to share his concern. It sounded valid. Was I, in fact, distracting people from the Bible rather than illustrating it?

By the sixteenth month of my new ministry, I was in the midst of what might be called preaching paranoia: Should I use sermon outlines? Should I tell that humorous story, or should I scrap it? How personal should I make my descriptions and illustrations?

Every time I used a study outline, I found myself looking at Ted. Every time I told a joke, I had to resist looking to the left side of the congregation to see if Bob was giving me a sanctified scowl. Whenever I mentioned a name, I was wondering if Jerry was moving into his fantasy world. I wanted to be a good preacher, especially to avoid anything that might hurt the communication process.

The situation came to a head when one man took me aside.

"Pastor," said Don, "sometimes I wonder how sincere you are when you preach. A man of God ought to go into the pulpit with fear and trembling, but last Sunday just before you were to preach, I saw you smiling at somebody in the congregation."

I remembered the incident immediately. During the hymn before the sermon, I looked up from the hymnal and caught a smile from my wife. I smiled back and kept singing that hymn of praise.

To assure Don of my sincerity, I explained my weekly preparation process. Throughout the week I studied, completing my sermon by Thursday. The message would be restudied on Friday. On Saturday evening I would go to the church and preach the sermon in the empty sanctuary. Saturday night after returning home, I would again review my outline. At home early Sunday morning, I would again read the text and go over my remarks. During Sunday school, I would spend the last half hour in prayer and study for the message. Just before the service, our staff would meet in the prayer room to pray together that God would be honored through the worship and preached Word. If that wasn't sincerity, I'm not sure what was.

As we talked, an interesting thing happened: rather than creating further introspection, the very nature of Don's comment broke the cycle of pastoral paranoia. I knew my motives, and I knew my preparation. If the smile offended him, then I was sorry. I could suck on dill pickles before I ascended the chancel, but I doubt if that would please everybody. It was the ridiculousness of his comment that freed me to realize I can't please everyone. Many people loved the study outlines, many responded to appropriate humor, and many were drawn to involvement through personal illustrations.

That turnaround in the sixteenth month of my ministry has remained decisive. As I reflect, and as other pastors have shared with me similar experiences, several conclusions emerge that can help us cope when we are criticized.

Live for Christ, Not Ministry

For me the ministry was my life. I loved the church, not because I felt it was a perfect institution, but because I knew it to be God's vehicle for spiritual maturity. My time and energy, then, were given to the church.

I didn't punch out at night; often I brought work home with me. The church was on my mind even as I slept. The pains of people and the details of the program did not stop at 5 P.M. on Friday.

The loop never closed. As soon as one sermon was given, a new one was already on the drawing board with, at most, a six-day deadline. There were always people who needed to be visited and counseled. There were additional programs to be started and staff to be trained.

And weekly, an "emergency" of one sort or another would demand my complete attention. The sound system failed one week; a custodial vacancy had to be filled another; the baptismal tank, which was to be used Sunday, had a rare culture growing in it.

When was enough enough?

Yet the busier I became with church ministry (most of which was good), the less consistent I was in spiritual disciplines. The ministry was my life, but something wasn't right. The joy of the Lord, the joy of true spiritual service, was disappearing.

One morning while reading in Philippians, the importance of a familiar verse in chapter 3 again challenged my priorities: Paul's desire was to know Christ. The thought occurred to me, *For what shall it profit a minister if he oversees home Bible studies, club programs, church services, youth ministries, ten committees, and preaches — if he loses his own soul, or at least his affection for and close walk with his Savior?*

The loop will never be closed — that's just the nature of ministry. I decided, though, that I would have to manage better the ministry demands and opportunities, and not let them consume me. Christ, not ministry, must be my life.

Maintain a Healthy View of Depravity

The body of Christ is composed of people who have two natures. While we can rejoice that Christians have been regenerated by the Holy Spirit, there remains within each believer the pull of the old self. At any given moment an individual can be following the influence of the Spirit or following the selfish, sometimes ugly behavior of the old self. If you're going to survive in the ministry, you have to have a healthy understanding of human depravity.

One of my former associates learned this lesson quickly one Sunday morning in the church boiler room. A few of us had gathered in the prayer room just prior to the morning worship service when Rick came in looking like a dog that had just been beaten. I asked what was wrong. He filled us in.

While passing through a class in the basement, he was asked to step into the boiler room, away from people, because Jerry wanted to "share something" with him. (I should have warned him about situations that began with "I want to share something with you," especially if the words "in love" are added.)

Once inside the small cubicle, Jerry poured out how he felt Rick had failed him during his convalescence from surgery. Although Rick and I had both visited him and phoned more than once, it wasn't enough for Jerry. The nature of the speech, the intensity of his body language, and his full six-foot-four-inch frame completely devastated Rick.

While much of the criticism we receive is valid and beneficial, a lot of flak will be generated because the old nature within people is not yet eradicated.

We continually try to feed and encourage the new self. At the same time we should never be caught by surprise that, at any given moment, someone might behave with the ugly, hurtful behavior of the old self. That simply reminds us our job is not yet finished.

Regular, Systematic Evaluations

Proverbs 12:15 states, "The way of a fool seems right to him, but a wise man listens to advice." While some criticism might be amiss, some criticism may be very much on target. In order for that constructive criticism to reach my ears, I asked for systematic evaluations of my ministry. Regularly scheduled assessments help avoid stress-producing showdowns.

Every three years, our board of elders reviewed the eleven points of my job description. On each item they offered commendations and recommendations. They spent a couple of sessions alone together and then two to three hours with me.

As they gave their assessment, I listened, interrupting only to clarify what they were saying. Sometimes I took notes on the printed evaluation they provided, and the printed evaluation and my notes then served as a springboard for me to later discuss on their observations and concerns.

A systematic evaluation gives people permission to express positive and negative feelings about my ministry. If this vehicle for sharing criticism was not provided, then by default I would be encouraging people to share their views merely among themselves — a sure formula for pastoral paranoia.

Allowing for Different Tastes

I prize the office of pastor, if for no other reason than it puts me at the center of the Christian family called the church. That's also the reason the pastorate can be so difficult.

Most parents have difficulty keeping their children from each other's throats. Husbands and wives have their share of disagreements. But put one hundred of these families together in one collective church family with the pastor at the center — well, he or she is in for some interesting times.

And many of those times, when conflict seems at its worst, it's simply a matter of taste: some members of the family like things one way and some another. But like families, they can find themselves squabbling fiercely.

Some people like formal worship, others informal. Musically, some appreciate Bach; others prefer Maranatha. Some enjoy a challenging cognitive sermon, while others like the walls to shake with the threat of fire and brimstone.

Like many pastors, at first I wanted to please all the people all the time, and I took comments about people's preferences too seriously. But then I realized that in many instances, people's criticisms are nothing more than matters of taste.

Since that realization, I've been less unhappy about those who are not always happy. In fact, if someone moves to another church, it often proves beneficial to both them and us.

Providing an inclusive and diverse program is important. On the other hand, realizing that people have different tastes has helped me weather criticism.

I was visiting an elderly man one Monday morning when he said, "Pastor, yesterday I heard three sermons. It's funny. I can remember Jerry Falwell's outline and Charles Stanley's outline, but I can't remember yours."

My first reaction was to get defensive, to wonder what he was trying to communicate, to doubt I was doing a good enough job. I finally decided, though, that the statement was not offered as a specific suggestion. It was hardly constructive criticism. It was just a thoughtless statement from one of my dual-natured (or is that duel-natured?) people.

I can't compete with many famous preachers, and if this man remembered their sermons better than mine, so be it. I'm continually trying to improve my preaching, but my style, even if it were to be perfected some day, is never going to satisfy everyone.

Since I can't please all the people all the time, for God's glory I've begun to use the personality, talents, and gifts he has given me to serve wholeheartedly in the church to which he has called me. And with that, I find myself looking back less at those carping and more ahead to the One who is leading.

— *John Cionca*

> My goal is to take away the emotional flash point by
> affirming truth, not by castigating falsehood and
> wrongdoing. Truth delivered in the right spirit will
> eventually win the day.
>
> — Edward Dobson

CHAPTER FOUR
Preaching the Controversial Sermon

A few years ago I preached about alcohol. I raised an issue that had never been addressed in the history of the church. It had been ignored perhaps because there are two views on drinking in our congregation.

Some people in our church want the Bible to say, "Don't drink." Others, the larger element, have no problem with light social drinking.

After the sermon, as you can well imagine, one group was angry because it felt I had opened wide the door to drinking. These people thought all the young people were going to go out and get drunk.

Another large group of people said, ironically, "Boy! You've sure made us feel uncomfortable about using any alcohol."

That's the nature of preaching on controversial topics — it can create even more controversy! Church controversy is inevitable, and sometimes it's the preacher who generates it.

Why Preach about Controversial Subjects?

I don't particularly like preaching on controversial topics. I've learned that most of the time when I do, there's a price to pay — I'm bound to make somebody angry. Sometimes I feel that in raising issues, I'm threatening the very existence of my ministry or the church's ministry.

So why do I do it?

● *To fulfill an obligation to the truth.* I have an obligation to respond honestly to issues that impact the church. To ignore them is to ignore the reality of the world in which people live.

For example, not long ago, our church rethought its views on marriage, divorce, and remarriage, essentially changing what our church had practiced for 60 years. We had to face these issues in light of the rising divorce rate in the last couple of decades. As a consequence, I had to preach on these subjects, to make clear our church's new policies.

Women in ministry is another issue at the center of controversy in churches today. To ignore it is beyond comprehension to me; it's one of the key issues about which people are confused. There are a lot of women in high levels of management who are asking questions about women in ministry. They have a right to hear legitimate, reasonable answers from the church.

For me to ignore such realities is to be less than concerned about the truth. Scripture has something to say about every great issue of the day. It's part of my calling to speak forth what I believe the Bible to be teaching.

● *To fulfill an obligation to people.* After I once spoke about the need to forgive others, I received a note that said, "I'm 18 years old. When I was 14, my dad raped me, and I got pregnant. Now I have a 4-year-old kid. And every time I look at the kid, I think of my dad. So how can you sit up there and tell me to forgive? My dad still denies he ever even touched me."

It's not just issues that I'm concerned about but also the people who struggle with those issues. Women are wondering how to respond to feminism, teenagers to sex, businesspeople to ethics, and on and on. Individuals are struggling with controversial issues. If I want to be their pastor, if I want to help them in their Christian walk, I will have to deal from the pulpit with their concerns.

Keeping Conflict Out of the Controversy

I've discovered my own attitudes affect how my message is received. The spirit in which I deliver my sermon is often reflected in the response people give me. I've discovered several things that have helped me minimize needless antagonism.

● *Get the view from the pew.* I've found it helpful when dealing with controversial issues to soak in the viewpoints and feelings of those who differ from me. But I've got to get out of my study to do that.

Often after I've prepared my sermon, I sit in the auditorium and try to put myself in the place of people who will be sitting in that pew on Sunday. 1 try to imagine what they went through over the last week, what their relationships are like, and what they're struggling with. I keep asking myself, "What difference will this sermon make? How will they see it? What conclusions will they draw from it?"

Of course, there's nothing like direct contact with my people to keep me in touch with their views. In our Saturday night service, which is for unchurched people, we have a period for questions and answers at the end of every talk. People write questions related to the topic for the service, and I try to respond to them. Doing that week after week gives me a window to see where people are coming from and what they're really thinking.

Best of all, I get the view from the pew by hearing personally, after worship and during the week, the dilemmas that my people face.

One man in my congregation worked on a business venture for a year and a half and stood to make a six-figure commission. Then at the last minute, somebody at the bank got involved and bypassed him, violating the law in the process. He came to me and asked me what he should do.

"Do I sue," he asked, "or is God trying to tell me to let go of all this money?"

It's one thing to preach platitudes about materialism; it's another thing to answer a direct question: "How does your sermon apply to me when I've been cheated out of money I can't afford to lose?"

When I know the real dilemmas that my people face, my preaching is not only more realistic, it's more compassionate, and needless controversy, due to a simplistic judgmental spirit, is avoided.

• *Affirm truth more, condemn error less.* In my sermon on drinking, I was careful not to impose false guilt about drinking. I merely explained some of the reasons I abstain. I talked about the drug and substance problem in our country, about research that shows some people to be genetically predisposed to alcoholism, and about the terrible pain that alcoholics go through.

"For all those reasons," I said, "I've chosen not to drink."

I also made sure that my approach was thoughtfully reasoned and that I was fair to each side's position. My goal is not to split the difference between factions or to find politically safe ground. My goal is to take away the emotional flash point by affirming truth, not by castigating falsehood and wrongdoing. Truth delivered in the right spirit will eventually win the day.

• *Make careful use of surprise.* Sometimes, when used appropriately, surprise provides the spark to drive a point home without alienating people.

When I preached about drinking, I set people up. I listed from the Bible those who abstained from wine because they wanted to be unique and separate, such as those under a Nazaritic vow and John the Baptist. And as they listened, all the non-drinkers were thinking, *This is great!*

Then I said, "Now let me show you some who didn't abstain."

And I immediately mentioned Jesus. People told me later that when I did this, they were compelled to listen to what I was going to say next.

I can't use surprise, however, simply to shock people. It must be scriptural in intent or content, and it must be pastoral, seeking in love to speak the truth. When I sense I'm not motivated properly, I'll drop the surprise.

• *Be fair to opposing views.* When preaching on controversial matters, it's often a temptation to treat unfairly those whom we oppose.

For example, I once preached on Jesus' statement, "Unless you eat the flesh of the Son of Man and drink his blood, you have no life in you." Since about 10 percent of our Sunday morning congregation is Roman Catholic, I wondered how I could address the fundamental issues without attacking Catholics personally or labeling them as ignorant, unbiblical Christians.

So I read a great deal of Catholic theology on the subject. Then when I preached, I said, "Some biblical scholars interpret the passage like this . . ." And I explained the strongest argument from a Catholic position.

Then I said, "Now let me give you four or five reasons why I believe this passage ought to be interpreted this other way."

The Catholics thought it was wonderful. They said, "I never saw it that way. It makes sense!" They could respond positively because I didn't single them out. I treated them with respect. In fact, I hadn't even labeled their scholars or doctrine as "Catholic." Still the Catholics recognized what I was talking about.

Labeling, in fact, is a special temptation in controversial preaching. But I avoid it at all costs, and I encourage my listeners to avoid it as well.

In my sermon on drinking, after laying out my reasons for and against drinking, I said, "We may not be able to come to agreement about this issue. But let's do at least this much: let's not call each other 'legalists' and 'liberals,' but just 'brothers' and 'sisters.' "

• *Keep my ultimate focus on God, not people.* Although I want to be sensitive to people, I don't want to let their reactions control how I preach.

I went through a terrible episode a couple of years ago. In that case, it wasn't my preaching that caused the problem, but the actions of somebody else. Still, the situation elicited the same kind of emotions in me as when controversial preaching is involved.

A woman in the church came to see me and asked, "Have you been looking at me? Have you been making eyes at me while you're preaching?" She was convinced I was attracted to her.

"No, I don't even know who you are," I said. To head off the problem, I asked my wife and the woman's husband to join the woman and me for a counseling session. Afterwards, she admitted she had a lot of emotional problems and agreed to get professional help.

But she still continued to tell her friends that the preacher was making eyes at her. She'd sit way out in the congregation thinking, *When he preaches, he's giving me the eye. I can tell he's in love with me.*

I turned the problem over to the church board, asking them to deal with it, and I tried to relax, but every Sunday for about six months, whenever I came to the pulpit, I knew that woman was sitting out there somewhere, thinking I was loving her from a distance.

I became self-conscious as I preached. Every sermon was weighted with deliberate effort to be careful where I looked. I tried to lose myself in worship and focus on God, but most of the time it didn't work. I'd catch myself thinking, *I wonder where she's sitting. If I happen to notice her, I'll look to another section.* Everything I did was affected, and she severely limited my spontaneity.

After the service, I'd think, *Let's see. If I stand here to shake hands with people, will she and her husband come down this aisle?* I'd wonder, *What else is she saying to people?*

The whole experience taught me a terrific lesson about trusting my reputation and my effectiveness to God. Gradually I learned to speak freely even though I felt oppressed. Even while struggling with inner conflict, I found I could be faithful to the text. If the passage called for confident or joyful delivery, I could do that out of obedience, and God brought results regardless of what I felt inside.

As pastor I have to tell myself on occasion to put my feelings aside and be professional about fulfilling my responsibilities.

The Place and Use of Scripture

The Bible, handled correctly, also can keep me out of needless controversy. Scripture helps me zero in on what really matters and guides me in the way I approach people. Here's how I use the Bible whenever I face controversial issues.

• *Let Scripture determine which battles will be fought and when.* Especially during periods of conflict, my sermons must begin and end with Scripture. This is where expository preaching has kept me out of trouble.

I know that whatever crisis erupts this week, this coming Sunday I'm preaching the next sermon in my series from the Gospel of John or Romans or wherever I happen to be in the Bible. I don't allow myself to react, to let the events of the week unduly influence what I preach — I try to let the upcoming text do that. Like a governor on an engine, expository preaching helps me maintain a proper speed and not get carried away.

Expository preaching will, in its own time and place, address difficult topics. I preached on drinking, for example, simply because I was preaching an expository series through the Gospel of John. And there it was: Jesus turned the water into wine. People asked, "What kind of wine was it?" It was a legitimate question that needed to be answered. And because it was addressed in the context of expository preaching, people didn't feel like I was "dumping" on them.

• *Use Scripture to defuse emotional feedback.* A scriptural foundation also helps me deal with emotional feedback after the sermon. My defense to critics is, "If you can show me where I misrepresented the Bible, I'll correct it. Did I say anything unscriptural? Did I say anything wrong from the Bible?"

One woman heard on the radio the sermon about drinking. It troubled her because her son is an alcoholic. In fact, he was in church that Sunday. When he returned home, he said to her,

"Dobson said drinking is okay." So she called me up and blasted me.

"Every person killed by a drunk driver will be your fault," she said. "And the blood of people in this community will be on your hands."

But I said, "Now, tell me from the Bible what I said wrong."

"Well, that's not the point," she answered.

And I said, "That is the point."

I try not to defend myself (which is my tendency) or to get cynical. I simply try to keep coming back to the Bible.

• *Use Scripture in proportion to the issue.* Some churches are embroiled in battles over issues the Scriptures do not address. If the Bible allows room for various interpretations, I want my sermon to give space too.

For example, some people in our congregation want me to debate the merits of public, home, and Christian schooling. But I've retreated from that battle because I can't honestly see how the Scriptures make a hard case for any of the options. It seems to me that individuals will have to make that decision for their families on a human, not a scriptural level — based on preference and broad biblical principles, not biblical absolutes.

Naturally, which topics have strong biblical roots and which don't is a judgment each preacher has to make. But here are some principles that guide me:

1. *Defend Christian distinctives at all costs.* There are some absolutes of the Christian faith — those beliefs that distinguish a non-Christian from a Christian, the things on which we all must agree: the gospel of grace, the incarnation of Jesus, the centrality of Scripture, among others. There can be no disagreement on these without compromising the integrity of the church. So these are issues that must be addressed, directly and indirectly, from the pulpit regularly, even if they raise havoc.

2. *Preach convictions, but acknowledge other views.* Next are matters of conviction — beliefs we each hold about non-essentials.

As a congregation, we have established certain convictions

about such things as eschatology and dispensationalism and baptism. It is our conviction, for instance, that infants shouldn't be baptized; so we don't. But we don't rebaptize people who, as infants, were baptized and now wish to join our church.

Yet even though they're not biblical absolutes, convictions are legitimate topics for preaching. As pastor, I believe our church convictions, and I'm called upon to defend them. However, I always qualify what I say by adding that other sincere Christians may disagree with our convictions.

3. Hold preferences loosely. Finally, there are preferences. Our style of worship, for instance, is a preference. Dress and externals are all preferences to me. If I accept people with different convictions, there is no way I can judge people because of their preferences. The Bible allows room for a wide variety of preferences, and in my preaching on controversial subjects, I have to remind people of that from time to time.

In one sermon on Christian music, a hot issue in our church at the time, I acknowledged that some Christians are strongly against contemporary music. Then I pointed out that at one time all church music was contemporary and that we tend to forget that.

Then I dropped the bomb shell. I said, "I love contemporary music. I like Christian rock. Now this is only my opinion — it's not a scriptural absolute or even a conviction. It is a preference." Then to deal with the inevitable reaction, I granted that some of them would think I was crazy, even if I was pretty straight in other ways.

"It's fine for you to think that," I said, "as long as you don't judge me as being less spiritual because of my preference."

Then I reminded those on the contemporary side of the issue — who were feeling a little smug by this time — that they also must maintain a level of tolerance. I told them if they wanted to tell the traditionalists, "Get with the program," then they were being libertarian legalists. And I reminded them that we don't use hard-hitting contemporary music on Sundays. Our purpose is to enable and encourage everybody to worship God, not to prove we're free.

When Scripture is used appropriately, then, it can keep the waters of controversial preaching a little more calm.

Mistakes to Avoid

It wouldn't be controversial if an issue didn't engage our emotions. That's the nature of conflict and disagreement. And though I want to be involved emotionally with what I do and say, I cannot permit myself to be carried away by the intensity of the moment; otherwise I jeopardize my ability to lead my congregation.

With a clear head then, I guard myself against several mistakes that can easily trip me.

● *Acting like the final authority.* Twenty years ago, a lot of churches felt that if the pastor said it, it had to be true. But this is a different generation. People won't respond to an appeal unless the preacher makes a good case for it, and even then they're going to be skeptical. If I come across as an authoritarian, I'm not going to have an opportunity to be heard. People will resist me. I can't get away with simply saying, "The Bible says, 'Don't drink,' " or "The Bible says, 'Women, be submissive.' "

In fact, I regularly tell my congregation, "You have an obligation not to believe what I tell you from the pulpit unless you can prove it from Scripture yourselves. I'm not trying to tell you what to believe; I want to help you interpret and apply the Bible honestly. I'm human; I make mistakes. Therefore the believer's responsibility is to judge what I say with the help of the Holy Spirit and the Scriptures."

● *Making private matters public.* Some internal church controversies do not belong in the public eye. They should be addressed behind closed doors, not from the pulpit. Bringing them out into the open only makes these conflicts worse.

So whether the issue is between angry individuals or church factions up in arms, we try to solve the problem at the level where it really exists. We try never to make a problem more public than it ought to be.

If it's an issue of interpreting the church constitution or some procedural matter, for example, we deal with it at the board level; the elders are the ones responsible to deal with that. If it is aggrieved parties in the congregation, we deal with it at that level and do not make it a public issue.

• *Belittling people's experiences.* Sometimes I'm tempted to downplay or even make fun of people's experiences if they threaten to undermine what I'm trying to teach. But experiences, no matter how contrary to what I'm teaching, are real, and they must be treated seriously.

During our Saturday night service, one of the notes I received during the question and answer time read, "My mother died, and my dad remarried, and he married a bitch." It went on and on: "When she dies, my greatest joy will be to stand at her grave and sing the Doxology."

People in the room began to snicker, but beneath the sarcasm of this note was a lot of pathos. I started to respond, but the author of the note spoke up from the audience.

"That was my question," he said, "and I didn't appreciate people snickering and laughing. I've been going through hell." All of a sudden the nice, neat theological principle we were discussing — forgiveness — wasn't so nice and neat anymore. It was still valid but not so simple.

I talked directly to him: "I apologize for those who laughed," I said. "It's not funny; you're right. And I want to thank you for your courage to stand up to it."

Then I talked more about forgiveness and letting go.

I went down and hugged him, and a bunch of people came and hugged him. I told him forgiveness was not just a single act but a life-long process of letting things go.

So he's been working at it since. He claims our Saturday night meetings are the only genuine religious experiences he's had, and we're the only church where he has felt loved and accepted.

I can't escape the inevitability of controversy in the church. Preaching, in fact, generates healthy controversy by itself. But when done in the right way, it can not only prevent things from getting worse, in the long run it can make the church better.

How much firepower is appropriate in a church fight? No
Geneva Convention has established any rules.

— Marshall Shelley

CHAPTER FIVE

Surviving a Power Play

Church conflict can take many forms. Sometimes it's just random
sniping — isolated complaints, but dangerous enough to keep you always
wary: "I have some concerns about our church, Pastor, which I've been
sharing at our prayer group."

Other times, the conflict is confined to border skirmishes — different
groups squabbling over "turf" — who gets to decide the Sunday school
curriculum or who gets priority in using the multipurpose room?

Other times, however, the conflict is all-out war or a well-planned
palace coup. Nothing less than the ouster of the pastor will satisfy the

opposition, and nothing less than a groundswell of popular support will keep the pastor in place.

Perhaps the best way to illustrate the way such conflict can escalate from one stage to the next is simply to tell one pastor's experience, then to allow him to reflect on what he learned.

I remember sitting more than once with the pastor who told the following story (in which the names have been changed). In the midst of the conflict, the strain visible in his face belied his words, with which he tried to be positive and upbeat. Only after the war was over did he reveal most of the details.

* * *

Pastor Charles Westerman was surprised when Jack Kenton was picked by the nominating committee for the position of board chairman. Only six months earlier, Charles had heard via the grapevine that Jack was thinking of leaving Morningside Chapel. Charles remembered several occasions when Jack had mentioned, "Pastor, the church isn't as friendly as it used to be; we're growing too fast to keep up with everyone."

Charles agreed with that not unusual observation, but he thought it was a nice problem to have. The church, just outside Harrisburg, Pennsylvania, had grown in the last two years — lots of people drifting in and staying, others drifting off, blaming the church's size for an impersonal feel. Charles was doing what he could to foster intimacy through Sunday school classes and small groups, but he also knew larger churches would naturally "feel" different from small ones.

One of Jack Kenton's closest friends, Clarence Porter, was chairman of the nominating committee, and Judy Kenton, Jack's wife, also sat on the committee. The Porters and the Kentons were among the "old guard," charter members of the church. They'd apparently convinced a majority of the twelve-member committee that Jack would make a good board chairman.

When he first heard about the nomination, Charles spoke with Clarence Porter: "I've worked with two board chairmen in the five years I've been here, and I had a close relationship with both of them. I've had lunch once or twice with Jack, but we're not particularly close. We don't always see eye to eye. I'd prefer another candidate."

"Jack's a good man, Pastor," Clarence said. "He's a spiritual leader in his home, a student of Scripture, and he has memorized more verses than most people have read. He knows our church and its needs. I think he'll work well with the board. Besides, he's already accepted the nomination. If we take his name out now, he'll know someone objected, and he'll probably leave the church."

Charles suspected Clarence would tell Jack who the "someone" was. In fact, he suspected a bit of a power play by the old guard to limit his leadership, to put the brakes on the church's growth, to move the attention away from new people and back to the core group.

He didn't want to alienate the charter members of the church. They were an important part of the flock and deserved to be heard. Yet Charles felt part of the church's mission was to reach out continually. Jack would undoubtedly resist that.

Nor did Charles want to veto the twelve members of the nominating committee. He honestly didn't want to stack the board, and he didn't want to be accused of running a dictatorship. After all, he was pleased with the rest of the slate. Why be picky over one nomination?

So he committed himself to serving with Jack and making him a successful board chairman. From the pulpit, Charles thanked the nominating committee for their "strong choices" and watched the entire slate unanimously voted in.

Preliminary Sparring

The next breakfast meeting with Jack seemed to go well, both men agreeing to work together and Jack quoting his verse of the week, Psalm 26:8 — "Lord, I have loved the habitation of thy house, and the place where thine honor dwelleth" — but Charles was slightly uncomfortable with Jack's tone.

"He said he hoped he could help bring more depth to our

ministry," Charles confided to his wife. "He said he'd be praying for revival in my life and the lives of our staff. You can't argue with that, but he definitely puts you on the defensive. It feels like spiritual one-upmanship."

Despite their promise to work together, Charles and Jack were butting heads from the first board meeting. The air quickly became thick with tension and distrust. Jack had a way of questioning motives and intentions, especially regarding growth.

"Are you sure you're not just trying to build an empire?" he asked Charles more than once.

Dumbfounded, Charles replied, "No, I don't want an empire, Jack. Neither do I want to limit what the Spirit can do."

Jack continued to voice his suspicions. Anything that suggested enlargement — renting space for new Sunday school classes, rearranging the Christian education offices, hiring a part-time secretary — Jack was against.

"Why should we try to attract more people when we're not doing that great a job with those we've already got?" he asked.

He vehemently opposed a plan to relocate so the church could build a larger building; he persuaded a majority of the board and defeated the plan. He refused to help select an architect to draw up plans for enlarging the existing facility, but this time the board outvoted him eleven to one.

That was the first of many eleven-to-one votes. Even though he was outnumbered, Jack's Luddite assaults often caused the board to delay votes, because they hoped to reach consensus. They rarely did, though, and issues were bogged down for weeks.

Charles continued to meet with Jack once a month for breakfast. Jack complained, "I don't like the way you make unilateral decisions. I hear you're going to California in July to speak at a conference for a week. You never cleared that with me."

"I don't work for you," Charles said. "I don't even work *for* Morningside Chapel. I work *with* Morningside Chapel. I'm self-employed — look at my IRS form! I submit myself to the board of elders and the church, but I'm not an employee. I'm an ordained minister, charged with shepherding this flock. Some of these personal ministry decisions are mine."

Jack wouldn't buy it. "I think you have a spiritual problem, Charles. I don't think you're the man for this church. If you had the gift of discernment, you could see that this church needs more depth, that it needs revival. Have you been praying for revival in your own life?"

"Yes, I have been . . . daily."

Actually, thought Charles, *I should have said nightly.* Most nights he had been waking up at 2 A.M. — tossing and turning till 4 or 5 — praying and worrying about the direction of the church, asking God to show him how to resolve the tensions, trying to think of new angles that would help.

Night after night, he pondered, *Is there really a growing dissatisfaction, or am I just more sensitive because of Jack's constant harping? Is the church growing too fast? If people keep coming, what other alternative is there than trying to minister to them all?*

Is Jack right about my motives? I don't think so, but how can anyone know for sure? Of course, my ego feels better when the church is growing, but I can honestly say my greatest desire is that God be honored by what we do here.

Charles continued to lose sleep. He didn't know how to work with Jack. The monthly breakfasts were becoming an ordeal. Jack's persistent charge was that Charles wasn't spiritual enough to lead a church the size of Morningside. Bickering about spirituality, Charles concluded, is the most perverse kind of bickering.

Eventually, Charles told two of the elders about his deteriorating relationship with Jack. "We're like a husband and wife who bicker not only over the way the house is kept but also whether the other partner is fit company," he said. "There's no way a marriage can last if that keeps up. We've been stymied as a church, the spirit is gone from our board meetings, and we aren't acting with one accord. Eleven-to-one votes are becoming a Monday night liturgy. We're spinning our wheels. Am I the cause? Maybe if I resigned, the church would be more united."

The two elders said no, they didn't believe the situation was serious. "Eleven-to-one votes don't bother us, Pastor. And I'm sure you and Jack will eventually work things out. You just see things differently." Charles realized none of the board had heard Jack's private philippics. While he laid into Charles at the breakfasts, Jack's board meeting criticisms were more vague, less pointed, and only Charles felt their full impact because he knew what was behind them.

Charles could not tell how many others in the congregation Jack represented. At the breakfasts, Jack kept bringing up names of people he'd been talking to, and to hear him tell it, half the church was disgruntled.

Forced Errors

The tensions not only cost Charles sleep but also led to some errors of judgment.

"One Sunday I preached from 1 Corinthians 1:10 about 'Them,' those people in our lives who cause confusion and discord, especially in the church," Charles remembers. "I could tell by people's expressions that I'd completely lost them. Afterward my wife said, 'I think I know what you were saying, but I'm sure no one else did.' She was right. It was an oblique sermon, preached out of my own frustration, but the congregation wondered, *What in the world is he talking about?* They thought everything in the church was going fine."

In September, just after school started, the sanctuary was packed for both services, and people were sitting in folding chairs in the aisles. Charles asked all the members of Morningside to stand up. "Look around; see how crowded we are," he instructed. "Now you know why we're thinking of enlarging our sanctuary." With nervous laughter, people sat back down.

"It was tasteless," Charles now admits. "It was not something someone from Princeton would do. It was driving a thumbtack with a sledgehammer. I did it out of frustration, knowing we had to grow but very aware of the people opposed to growth."

In November, six months after Jack had taken office, the hostilities escalated. Early one Thursday morning, Charles was sitting in the restaurant, waiting for Jack to arrive. He was sipping coffee over the sports page when Jack tapped him on the shoulder. "Can I see you outside?" he asked.

Strange request, Charles thought as he followed Jack outside. *He's a busy man, but if he can't stay for breakfast today, why didn't he call or just say so at the table?*

Once outside, however, Jack angrily turned on the pastor. "I've lost all respect for you, Charles. You're no spiritual leader, and I don't think I can even talk with you anymore. It's a waste of time for us to keep meeting for breakfast. We don't get anything accomplished because you don't understand what the people need."

Charles was stunned but managed to say, "Maybe you're right, Jack. I've thought for some time now that we needed to take this matter of my leadership to the board and let them decide."

"If you do that, I'll resign, and the whole church will know you forced me out." Jack turned, got into this car, and drove off. Charles was left standing alone. *This is ridiculous,* he thought. *We're arguing about who's more spiritual, and we can't act like Christians and share a meal together.*

Should he take this to the board? If he forced the board to decide between him and Jack, Charles was confident the board would back him, but that could also split the church. Who could tell how many of the old guard would follow Jack out the door? He didn't want to call Jack's bluff. Without any better ideas, he finally decided to do nothing and pray for a miracle of reconciliation.

The Betrayal

At the next board meeting, the issue of the youth pastor took preeminence. Rob Runyon simply wasn't a youth pastor. The high schoolers were not attracted to him — with 150 names on the roll, Sunday school attendance had dwindled from 75 to 40, and Wednesday night youth group attracted 30. Rob's wife resented him being out evenings or off on weekend retreats, and he was discovering youth ministry can't be done nine to five. Even Jack said, "We need to confront the young man; he's really choosing the wrong career."

So, in a rare unanimous vote, the board made the difficult but necessary decision of asking for the youth pastor's resignation. As distasteful as any firing is, Charles was relieved that at least he and Jack finally agreed on something. The Christian education board approved the action, Charles received Rob's resignation, the situation was explained to the staff, and Charles was confident that all the proper procedures had been followed.

But how to announce it to the congregation? The board felt a brief announcement from the pulpit wasn't adequate. By consensus, the board decided that after the Sunday evening service a meeting should be held with those most affected — the high schoolers and their parents — to explain the situation. Charles was designated to make the explanation.

That night two hundred teens and parents packed the chapel. Rob hadn't been able to attract many high schoolers, but when he was let go, several began grumbling about the abruptness of it all. Charles hoped to calm the waters.

After explaining that Rob's gifts were in other areas, that the church wished him well as he sought the Lord's direction for his life, and that he would be paid for the rest of the school year, Charles asked if there were any questions or comments.

Immediately Jack stood up. "Yes, I'd like to ask a question."

Charles wondered what he didn't already know about the situation.

"I think you presented only part of the truth about Rob's situation," Jack began. Charles felt anger begin to smolder. Was Jack calling him a liar?

"Isn't it true that Rob was let go because he wasn't attracting enough kids? It seems to me he was trying to run a quality program for the few. He was at my house last week, and we had a small group over to pray for him, and he told me the goals he'd had for the group. He had a core of thirty on Wednesday nights. You can't develop a huge following in just a year and a half, nor perhaps should you. Isn't it better to build a solid ministry with thirty kids rather than chase after a hundred on the fringe?"

While Jack was making his speech, Charles was feeling his temperature rise. *Why is Jack pretending he wasn't in on the decision to let Rob go? What's he trying to do? Embarrass me? Start a mutiny? He's publicly contradicting me.* The hostility that had been building up for six months suddenly exploded.

"All right, Jack, you win. Farewell, friend!" Charles said bitterly and walked from the room, slamming the door, and leaving the teens and parents speechless. As far as he was concerned, he had quit Morningside Chapel. He was fed up, tired of the battle. Let someone else knock himself silly against this brick wall.

The Measure of the Opposition

No sooner had he gotten home than Dan Moran, his associate pastor, and two of the board members knocked on the door, wanting to know what was going on. They were confused. They had talked with Jack after the meeting, and he was calling for the pastor's resignation. "If the pastor doesn't exercise any more self-control than that, he doesn't have the spiritual qualifications necessary to lead us," he had said. The elders said they were having an emergency meeting the next night to discuss the situation, and they wanted to have all the facts.

Charles explained the whole story, beginning with the discomfort at the nomination, the early tensions, the blowup at breakfast, everything.

"I guess we made a mistake agreeing to the meeting with the parents tonight. You don't explain a firing publicly; you make the decision, take the heat, and let it pass," he concluded. "But tonight isn't the real issue. The real issue is the direction of this church —are we going to reach out and continue to grow, or are we going to shut down our growth to concentrate on those we've already got?"

The whole board, minus Jack, met with Charles on Tuesday night. On Thursday night, minus Charles, they met with Jack. On Friday night, the board met with both of them.

Jack raised the issue of his authority as board chairman: "The pastor isn't in submission to me." They discussed what it meant to be in subjection to one another. The authority of the chairman, the board, and the pastor were argued, and delineations were made. After two hours, Charles agreed to submit to the board's authority, and Jack agreed that the chairman was "first among equals" on the board and that he, too, would submit to the authority of the board as a whole.

But Saturday morning, Jack changed his mind. He called Charles, said the situation was intolerable, and that he was resigning. Charles said, "I'm sorry you feel that way," but he didn't try to change his mind. A congregational meeting was announced for Sunday night.

"I did not appear in the pulpit on Sunday morning," Charles says. "I had really blown my cool the previous Sunday night, so I went to the high school class and apologized. I did not use the name of our chairman, but I explained that frustrations in the ministry had been building up and that night they boiled over. I let them know I had acted badly and was sorry."

Sunday night, the church was packed for the congregational meeting. Rumors and questions had been circulating: Was the pastor resigning? Had the elders fired him? What was happening?

When the chairman's resignation was read, the crowd was silent, but the more perceptive ones knew a power play had been attempted and failed. The vote to accept the resignation was overwhelming: 498 to 12.

The Kentons and the Porters both stopped attending the church, but almost none of the rest of the old guard did. In the months following, congregational votes on expansion issues passed by 80 percent approval, but the remaining 20 percent, while complaining, did not leave the church. Today, people continue to debate ways to make such a large church personal, but the ministry continues to grow. The old guard no longer threatens to leave.

"I was fortunate," Charles concludes. "I made some tactical errors and bad judgments, but I survived because our staff was well-liked and our vision for the church was generally accepted. But if Jack Kenton had been able to gain more of a following, he could have split the church."

Reflections from the War Room

When two groups differ over the direction of the church,

tensions naturally rise as they each try to gain the upper hand. If the issues are significant, both sides know the consequences of losing — the church won't be the same again. All the ingredients are there for a firefight — with all the resulting casualties.

Even the New Testament church knew the pain of living as a house divided until some key issues were settled.

In Galatians 2, Paul describes his power struggle with some "false brothers" over the expectations laid on Gentiles who were converting to Christianity.

It was theological, emotional, and ecclesiastical hard ball. When the clash was over, the church was split, the winners — Paul, Peter, Barnabas, and Silas — going on to take the lead, write the New Testament, and turn an empire upside down. The losers faded into history, nameless characters known only as Judaizers.

The power struggle ended, we all agree, with the right side on top. The essence of the gospel was at stake. Wouldn't it have been different, and tragic, if the wrong group had won? Yes, some wars have to be fought — and won.

Churches today have power struggles just as brutal. Most of them deal with matters of practice, not belief, but the hostilities aroused are as heated as if the essence of the gospel were at stake. One church nearly split over whether to accept a wealthy member's designated gift of a new organ or to sell it and give the money to the poor.

A significant issue — but worth fighting for? Worth splitting a church for?

How much firepower is appropriate in a church fight? No Geneva Convention has established rules.

A healthy congregation doesn't allow one or two members to set the church's direction or change its mission. Neither is the solution open warfare.

What can we learn from the power struggle at Morningside Chapel and the multiplied thousands of others like it? Pastors who have won and those who have lost similar struggles agree on several key principles.

• *Face the wind.* Boat captains in a storm know that running before the gale can force them onto rocks. When faced with political typhoons, the best chance for survival is facing them directly.

Charles Westerman let himself be tossed by the wind, and his frustration built to the point of losing emotional control, and it almost landed him on the rocks.

"I think it was Napoleon who said, 'Never let your enemy choose the battlefield,' " he reflects. "I don't consider Jack Kenton an enemy, but I certainly let him choose the battlefield. I lost control. If necessary, I should have offered my resignation before the board, not before two hundred people already upset over the youth pastor.

"I should have taken our disagreement to the board from the beginning, certainly at the point when he refused to have breakfast with me. Instead of my losing sleep, they could have helped me gauge the strength of the opposition. If I was out of line, they could have corrected me. If he was wrong, they could have stepped in sooner."

● *Prevent church fights from becoming holy wars.* Nothing is bloodier than a religious war. Issues aren't just human squabbles; everything is elevated to eternal importance. Charles Westerman says, "How easy to forget that it was the Devil whose tactic in Genesis 3 was getting two people to believe 'You will be like God, knowing good and evil.' " How tempting even today to mistake our will for God's; how devilish to believe that disagreeing with me is disagreeing with God."

Despite the pop spirituality that says, "Every problem is a spiritual problem," not every disagreement is a clash between good and evil, between the divine and the demonic.

"I wish my church members could recognize that they're just having a barroom scrap," says a Bible church pastor. "Some people enjoy going out on Friday night and getting in a fight with the good ol' boys. You mix it up a while, but nobody holds it against anybody. But in the church, people have to justify their scraps, so they're determined to cast them as the spiritual versus the unspiritual."

The problems at Morningside, as bad as they were, did not escalate further because Charles finally decided not to turn his clash with Jack into a religious war. He recognized how incongruous it would be to fight about who was most spiritual. Although he was tempted not to, he managed to keep it in perspective.

A Massachusetts pastor learned the same lesson. He had just seen his church break ground for a new sanctuary, but the battle to get the congregation's approval had been costly, and the funding would be a continuing struggle. The next day he was in the hospital having x-rays for severe stomach pain. His youth pastor came to his bedside.

"I know what's bothering your stomach," the associate said, pausing and looking out the window. "You know, Pastor, this building isn't the greatest thing that's going to happen for the kingdom of God in Massachusetts this week."

"I needed that," the pastor said after his release. "The x-rays didn't show a thing, but my associate touched the problem directly. I realized our million dollar building wouldn't bring God's kingdom one inch closer. He might choose to honor it, but he doesn't need it, nor does he need any of our self-important efforts."

The pastor's stomach pain disappeared and has not returned.

● *Failure is not fatal.* Though it didn't happen immediately, Charles Westerman eventually left Morningside Chapel. He wasn't forced out, but the continuing guerrilla warfare had taken its toll. He felt he had to have a change of scenery.

Even if the worst happens — a power play succeeds, and a pastor is compelled to resign, whether out of frustration or the efforts of the opposition — that doesn't mean the ministry is over. Just as one dissident isn't the whole church (though at times the angry voice is deafening), so one pastorate is not an entire ministry. Winston Churchill once said, "Success is never final; failure is never fatal; it is the courage to continue that counts."

Pastors who survive church wars unscathed are a small minority; those who have left a pulpit under less than happy circumstances are legion.

"When I was about to be forced out of my church," says a Kansas pastor, "I was feeling sorry for myself until I talked with an old veteran missionary who was visiting our church. I told him my troubles, and he said, 'Phil, better men than you have been kicked out of a church. It's not the end of the world.' That was just what I needed."

That pastor, at 58 years old, is now happily ministering in

another congregation.

"It's doubtful that God can use any man greatly until he's hurt him deeply," said A. W. Tozer. In weakness, God's strength can be revealed. Joseph was jailed, David driven into hiding, Paul imprisoned, and Christ crucified. But even in defeat, God's servants are not destroyed. Part of the miracle of grace is that broken vessels can be made whole, with even more capacity than before.

Part 3
Understanding the
Conflict

> *The level of conflict has less to do with the problem than with people's reaction to it. Just because people are open and honest with each other doesn't mean that real differences do not exist. Of course, as the stakes get higher, so does the possibility of more intense conflict.*
>
> — *Speed Leas*

CHAPTER SIX

The Varieties of Religious Strife

Conflict comes in many colors.

We normally know it as red, fiery hot: shouting matches, withdrawn pledges, fired pastors, split churches. This type of conflict burns everyone it touches.

But conflict also comes in blue, as cool and calm as a placid mountain lake. Issues are moved, seconded, debated calmly, and voted upon. People walk out of meetings "losers" but not bitter or angry.

Other conflict is green, contributing to the growth of a congregation. Some is black, foreboding doom for the church. Some is an amorphous gray, uncertain and undecided but enveloping the church like fog.

So when we talk about church conflict, we're talking about many things. And when we talk about dealing with conflict, we need to recognize the specific color of conflict we're dealing with.

Analyzing the Levels of Conflict

In my consulting work, I see at least four types, or levels, of church conflict. In each level of conflict, two major factors give me clues about the amount of difficulty a church is facing: the objectives of the parties involved and the amount of distorted thinking.

By "objectives" of the parties I mean their goals — what they are trying to accomplish. In lower-level conflicts, parties usually stay focused on the problem or difficulty. In higher-level conflicts, the goal of the parties shifts to trying to hurt one another or gain control.

By "amount of distorted thinking" I mean this: as people become more anxious or frightened, it becomes more and more difficult for them to think clearly about what is actually going on. They have a hard time assessing how much the church is threatened by the other party.

The clarity of people's thinking, of course, is seen in their use of language: If the words they use are broad, diffuse, and scattered (e.g., "The elders are being difficult" or "The pastor *always* does . . ."), the parties are at a higher level of conflict. The more specific the language ("The pastor hasn't preached a good sermon in four Sundays" or "I'm discouraged that the elders didn't approve my salary request"), the lower the level of conflict.

Also, the level of conflict has less to do with the problem than it does with people's reaction to it. Just because people are open and honest with each other doesn't mean that real differences do not exist. It is possible for people to be in low-level conflict even when important issues are at stake. Of course, as the stakes get higher, so does the possibility of more intense conflict.

In addition, most churches tolerate certain levels of conflict, even though the conflict is unpleasant. And it's not unusual for the conflict to rise to that level and hold there, not getting worse. Many churches seem to have internal governors that prevent the tension from escalating.

Finally, churches don't necessarily move neatly from one level of conflict to the next. Churches sometimes skip levels altogether as they move up or down through conflict.

Here, then, are the five levels of conflict most churches experience and the strategies that are best used at each level.

Level I: Predicaments

In Level-I conflict, the major objective of the parties is to solve the problem. Level-I disputants don't accuse people: "What's the matter with you?" They stay focused on the problem.

For example, in a Level-I controversy over the pastor's salary, the pastor and the personnel committee simply try to reach an agreement about the pastor's compensation. The pastor does not accuse the personnel committee of being stingy, and the committee does not charge the pastor with greediness. The goal of the participants is not to punish or to get control; the goal is to reach an agreement that will appropriately meet the financial needs of the pastor within the salary standards for the position and the available resources of the church.

Participants' language tends to be specific and clear: "I believe I need another $5,000 just to afford to live in this community" or "I don't know that we can afford that large of a raise since pledges fell short this year."

People find it easier to articulate what could be done: "Maybe if we adjusted my salary package, we could in effect get me that $5,000" and "You know, if we presented your concerns to the congregation, I think we could raise a few more pledges, which would put us over the top." People think clearly and feel confident speaking to the point.

By and large, the conflicting parties are open with one another about the problem. Neither party is frightened or suspicious of the other. Each assumes good will upon the part of the other, so neither party withholds information. The level of candor, in fact, is an excellent indicator of the level of conflict.

Because this level of conflict is handled so smoothly, some people don't see it as "conflict." But whenever people of different views try to work out an agreement, no matter how graciously they do so, you've got conflict. Conflict, then, is part of every church's life.

Furthermore, conflict at this level is valuable to a church — that's why many people don't even consider calling it "conflict." When conflicts remain at this level, a great deal can be accomplished: problems get solved, people understand each other better, relationships improve, trust is deepened.

Level II: Disagreement

In Level-II conflict, the objective of the parties has shifted slightly: each party becomes increasingly concerned about self-protection. Parties are still concerned about solving the problem, but they are especially concerned about coming out of the situation looking good.

Furthermore, the language that people use now becomes more generalized. One hears "I don't know if I trust the treasurer anymore" or "The pastor doesn't seem to be doing his job." Such descriptions leave the hearer wondering what the person is actually talking about. They may well be accurate descriptions (not distortions, which we will see in Level III), but they merely point in the direction of the problem; they don't tell you what it is.

Level-I statements, on the other hand, might be "The treasurer hasn't been giving me the monthly reports as I asked" and "The pastor hasn't made a hospital call in two months."

At Level II, people's language has a higher emotional content. Each party reveals their increasing tension: "The treasurer makes me pretty angry" and "I'm very disappointed with the pastor."

People at Level II begin to lose trust in the church leaders to help them get through the problem. They look elsewhere for help. They talk to others in the church about their concerns. They take their problems home and discuss them with spouses and friends.

This can become destructive, of course, but it can work for the good too, especially if people receive feedback that helps them deal constructively with the conflict. For example: the pastor talks with a colleague about his frustrations with the treasurer; his colleague tells him how he dealt with a similar problem in his ministry, and the pastor finds it works in his own setting as well.

Parties also begin withholding information at Level I. It's not that anyone is distorting the facts or lying, but not everything that might be relevant is shared.

For instance, when the pastor suggests to the treasurer that he wants a monthly report, he may omit the fact that not getting the report makes him anxious, even angry. When the member tells the pastor he needs to be more of a shepherd, she may omit mentioning her noticing his failure to visit Mrs. Jones when she was hospitalized overnight.

The parties believe, moreover, that if they are to resolve the problem, everybody will have to compromise. In Level-I conflict, the parties work toward a win-win solution. At Level II, that hope has been abandoned. People assume they'll have to settle for some kind of a tradeoff: for example, the pastor may believe the best he can do is get a treasurer's report only every other month.

At Level I, parties explore the inaccuracies of the other party's case simply to discern the facts. But parties in Level II are more interested in "scoring points," demonstrating their intellectual prowess in conflict. When a conflict shows signs of becoming a contest, though, moving toward a consensus becomes even more difficult.

As in Level-I conflict, this level should not disturb churches. This is another level of conflict typical to most churches, a level that with a little patience and planning can be turned to the good.

That can be done by:

— Helping each party understand the specific source of their frustration.

— Getting the parties to tell each other, in a gracious way, the facts as they see them and the emotions they are experiencing.

— Helping the parties find an amenable solution to the conflict.

Level III: Contest

At Level III, conflict has become a full contest: the "players" are less concerned about the problem or looking good; now they want to win, to get their way.

They've lost perspective on the issue. When looking at the larger picture of a conflict at Level I or II, people still see in the foreground the problem and possible solutions. At Level III, problems and solutions have moved to the background.

It is much more difficult, then, for people to see clearly and accurately what is actually going on, and their language reflects this. Several distortions are common:

• *Dichotomizing.* To dichotomize means to see things as right or wrong, black or white. There is little or no room to explore a variety of alternatives: "Either we make a special appeal this Sunday or the church will go out of business!" or "Either the youth pastor resigns or our family leaves!"

• *Universalizing.* We universalize when we make broad generalizations that do not accurately describe what is going on in the church. We tend to use words like *everybody, nobody, never,* and *always*:

"The pastor never calls on the older people in the congregation."

"This church is split right down the middle. Everybody has taken sides."

Naturally, universal statements are rarely true, and saying them distorts people's views even more.

• *Magnification.* When we magnify, we assume the other party has evil motives. We also imply that our motives are righteous:

"They don't give one whit about this church. They could care less if we had to close the doors."

"At least *I've* given my life to this congregation, trying to make it a mission-oriented fellowship."

● *Fixation on feelings.* This means focusing on people's feelings rather than the facts of the problem.

For example, a couple approaches the pastor after worship and says: "We know of several families who are unhappy about your leadership."

"What are they unhappy about?" the pastor replies.

"We don't know, but you had better take care of it."

When not connected to some description of people's unhappiness, such a statement simply scares others:

"If you don't know why I am upset, there's no point in telling you."

"I'm hurt at what you've done; too hurt to even talk about it."

In lower levels of conflict, people express their feelings ("I am unhappy"), but they usually continue with specifics ("The pastor didn't let us know he was going away on a retreat this week.")

At Level III, groups and coalitions begin to form. These groups are not yet factions, which emerge at Level IV, but people are beginning to talk with one another. They may not meet regularly, nor do they have clear leadership or a hierarchy, but others begin to notice their consanguinity. Parties may even be given names: "the dissenters," or "the old-timers," or "Pastor Smith's friends."

It becomes difficult to separate issues from persons. Personal attacks increase and take the place of talking about the problem: "Pastor Jones is just lazy!" or "The women's group is a bunch of gossips!"

It also feels as if a problem this big has to be somebody's fault — someone must take the blame and punishment. Dynamics of church life and the complexity of the issue are ignored: the problem is due to bad or difficult people.

In addition, members begin to try to influence one another through emotional appeals rather than rational arguments: "You don't seem to care about what is happening here" or "Look how bad everybody feels now. We've got to do something!"

Finally, people at this level dispute about who should initiate peace overtures: "No way am I going to meet with that committee until the chairman apologizes" or "I'd be happy to work it out, but the pastor needs to come to our meeting first."

Handling Level-III Conflict

Obviously, Level-III conflict corrodes a congregation. Decisions made at Level III, because they are based on seriously distorted thinking, will often create more problems than they solve.

In one California church of 130 members, an elder was furious with the pastor. He originally became upset over some things the pastor said in two sermons. Then he chafed at the pastor for changing the order of service. Those objections escalated into accusations of hypocrisy and arrogance.

When the elder board refused to take actions on his complaints, he threatened to send a personal letter to every member of the congregation, explaining his problems with the pastor. That would have "punished" the pastor by embarrassing him (the elder's main goal), and it would have split the tiny church in two. It was overkill.

The other elders quickly and decisively told him not to send his letter, and fortunately he did not.

In general, I want to reduce Level-III conflict to Level I or II. I can do that in the following ways:

● *Increase the amount of clear, direct communication between the parties.* This is the key to reducing conflict at Level III. I want parties to hear directly from each other what each of their concerns are. To do that, I need to get them together.

And I can get them together only if they feel safe with one another. To that end, I do the following:

— Clarify who will be there.

— Clarify the agenda.

— Clarify the ground rules.

When warring parties get this information ahead of time (even helping to determine it), they are much more willing to come and talk to one another, and they are more likely to reach agreement.

● *Help the parties explore areas of common agreement.* Before they look at their areas of disagreement, I will attempt to raise their level of hope. If the parties do not believe they have any common ground (or forget that whenever they get together) or see no possibility for advancing their concerns, the conversation will probably not go far.

● *Help the parties discover the deeper interest.* The concerns and solutions each party proposes may seem incompatible. However, behind each position may lie a range of interests that have not yet become conscious or been articulated. These deeper concerns can become the basis upon which other alternative solutions arise.

I once worked with a congregation with a conflict over the membership list. One staff member and several volunteers had for years kept the membership list on an Apple computer, although the church also owned an IBM for other office uses.

But one year, three other staff people went to receive computer training so that the church could keep financial records, data bases, and membership lists in a coordinated way. The program they were trained to use, however, was only IBM compatible.

Consequently, these people suggested that the membership lists be transferred to the IBM system, and that's when the Apple-list people started feeling they were losing control of their work — they thought they would not be able to access names as easily on the new system.

The people trained on the IBM system felt the Apple people were silly, and they began entering the 1,800 member names in their computer. Soon the church had two membership lists and a different group of people overseeing each one.

When I was called in, I met with each group separately to discuss what it was they really wanted. I also helped them look at the consequences of continuing to run dual membership systems. They each agreed to meet together to see if each party's needs could be addressed. We agreed on the ground rules and agenda for that meeting.

It turned out that neither group wanted the church to have dual membership records. In the end, the Apple people agreed to get training in the IBM system, and they began overseeing the entry and upkeep of the IBM lists, ensuring, they felt, the accuracy of the work. The IBM people provided overall management of the system.

Level IV: Fight/Flight

In Level-IV conflict the major objective of parties is to break the relationship, either by leaving or getting the other to withdraw. No longer is victory palatable; now the very relationship is a problem.

The language of people in Level IV is much like that of those in Level III. In addition, people express their dissatisfaction with non-verbal behaviors towards the "enemy" — not speaking, literally turning their backs, shouting, making obscene gestures, scowling, grimacing.

The focus of conflict shifts from issues and emotions to principles. The parties battle over eternal values — truth, human rights, justice. Often the issues being addressed by the parties are problems to solve, and workable solutions can be found. However, if the problems to solve are addressed as standard bearers for eternal principles, resolutions are extremely difficult to work out.

The strategies of those in Level IV are usually designed to end the relationship. Opponents are punished, shamed, and attacked in the hope that they will choose to go away.

In Level III, allies began to commiserate with each other in identifiable but loosely formed groups. In Level IV, strong leaders emerge, and the groups cohere. Members of the group defer to leadership, and the group makes plans as a group. Members begin to feel more powerful through their identification with their cause: there is a sense of cohesiveness, solidarity, and unity — exhilarating emotions indeed!

Allies, in fact, begin to identify more with their group than with the church. In fact, the good of the congregation as a whole takes second place to the good of the group's cause — or better, the good of the group becomes the good of the church. Parties push their own will at the expense of the whole, impugning the integrity of those not in the group, believing that those in opposition are essentially hypocrites.

Furthermore, the parties often attempt to enlist outsiders in their cause, and almost any outsiders will do: denominational officials, the press, neighboring pastors, conflict consultants. The expectation of people at Level IV is that when outsiders hear the complaints of the protagonists, they will surely want to join the cause and lend weight (or at least sympathy) to their side.

Level V: Intractable

At Level IV the parties are willing to let the other side live, if at a distance. At Level V, people believe the opposition is so evil and so virulent that simply getting rid of them will not do. The opposition must be punished or destroyed. Those at Level-V conflict believe, for the safety of the church, that the bad people must be disciplined so they can do no further damage.

For example, people at Level V are not satisfied with having the congregation fire a pastor. These people continue their battle at the denominational level, looking for ways to get the pastor defrocked.

Withdrawal from the conflict is next to impossible for parties at this level. Since one feels called by God to do these "mighty acts," pulling back would be seen as retreat, a demonstration that one does not truly believe.

Handling conflicts at Levels IV and V is beyond the scope of this book. In lower levels of conflict, getting someone or some group to come in from the outside (denominational officials, church consultants) can help. At Levels IV and V it is absolutely critical. The situation is out of control.

But things can get better. Recently I worked with an Episcopal Church where a powerful minority wanted to dismiss the pastor. They included about a third of the vestry (the board) as well as other leaders of the church school and choir — all influential leaders.

The pastor had not been there long, and the dissenters believed they had made a mistake in calling him. First they tried to get the bishop to remove the pastor — substantial Level-IV behavior. The bishop recommended they use a consultant.

I identified the concerns of the congregation, especially their concerns about the pastor's leadership style. I helped the larger membership see that the pastor's opposition, although composed of many pillars of the church, was small in number.

Since it was clear that the pastor had plenty of support in the congregation, the congregation decided to actively enlist the support of the dissidents in setting goals and a vision for the future.

In the process of identifying these goals, a couple of the dissenters decided to leave the church. But most stayed and worked on the goals and their relationship with the pastor.

Like most Level-IV conflicts, I would not say that everybody lived happily ever after. But there was a significant lowering of the level of conflict in the church.

It doesn't always work out this well, of course. And, as I said, most pastors shouldn't even get in the middle of a Level-IV or -V dispute. Still, as pastors are better informed about the exact nature of their churches' conflicts, the better are their chances of dealing with them redemptively.

> *Church conflict doesn't usually emerge from a single cause, and understanding the variety of causes is crucial to dealing with conflict.*
>
> *— Speed Leas*

CHAPTER SEVEN

Discerning the Causes

One California pastor found himself at odds with two men in his congregation. The problem was, well, that was the problem — this pastor couldn't figure out what exactly the problem was.

Certainly, a host of issues divided the pastor and the two men: They thought he preached too much on sin; he thought they lived by cheap grace. He thought clapping for the choir inappropriate in worship; they, as choir members, thought clapping a contemporary way of affirming the choir.

But some personal issues were involved as well: The pastor

preached a sermon about homosexuality, only to discover later that one of these men, who had a homosexual son, was hurt by the pastor's "insensitive" comments.

And then there was politics: These men had wielded a great deal of power in the church's short history. For some twenty years they had set the tone for the church: it would be an urbane, liberal, theologically diverse church. The pastor, however, was calling people to a more personal and Bible-centered faith.

The differences erupted one evening in a personnel committee meeting, of which these two men were a part. They lambasted the pastor, and the pastor tried to defend himself. Neither side budged an inch.

For weeks afterwards, the pastor tried to repair these relationships, but he couldn't figure out where the main problem lay, in theology, personalities, or politics.

What this pastor slowly realized was a basic truth of church conflict: conflict doesn't usually emerge from a single cause, and understanding the variety of causes is crucial to dealing with conflict.

As I've worked with congregations over the years, I've found that conflict has its roots in four areas: poor relationships, personal shortcomings (of people and pastor), unsolved problems, and congregational patterns of behavior. The first cause is discussed elsewhere in this book; let's examine the other three here.

Individual Shortcomings

We often assume that the church's problems are caused by the shortcomings of certain people — and that's all there is to it! That may not be all there is to it, but it's certainly true as far as it goes: many times it is cantankerous or ornery folk who make church life miserable.

I've found three shortcomings in people that cause church conflict.

● *Fear.* Many church conflicts begin when people become anxious about what is happening (or not happening) in the church. When anxiety, a certain level of which is healthy in organizations, turns into worry and fear, people begin to lose perspective about what is actually going on; then you get conflict.

In such cases, fear begins to act on the church as does pollen on a person who has hay fever. Hay fever sufferers have bodies that are hypersensitive to certain allergens. When those substances enter their bodies, their immune systems react so strongly that they become miserable. Their bodies' devices set up to protect them end up harming them.

So it is with fear. Sometimes we become aware of a problem and then overreact, so that the problem becomes worse than what we feared in the first place. When afraid, we sometimes lose our ability to think clearly and understand circumstances accurately. We act or make decisions that we later regret.

I worked with one pastor who had gotten wind of dissatisfaction among some of the elected church leaders. He assumed they would try to remove him from his position.

His response was swift and massive: he talked to many in the congregation, organizing groups to support him; he spoke with his bishop; he did not reappoint perceived opponents to positions of influence.

His reaction, however, was overkill given the level of concern brought by the "dissenters," and his response merely aggravated the dissatisfaction in the congregation.

Fortunately, two things happened that radically changed this pastor's reaction.

First, his bishop assured him that he would not allow the church to fire him. The bishop said, "You are guaranteed this position; there is virtually nothing that they can do to remove you from the church. Don't worry about it."

Second, the pastor and the dissatisfied members sat down together, and under the guidance of a skilled denominational official, discussed their cold war. The pastor learned that these people did not want him to leave the church; they simply had concerns about worship and administration.

● *Needs.* Sometimes our needs conflict with the needs of others, and that's when church conflict can begin.

Such conflict nettles all relationships. Recently, I was in the dumps because a church training program I had organized for a congregation had floundered. At the same time, my wife, a writer of computer manuals, had just been asked to write a sizable manual for a large computer company.

She was high and wanted to celebrate; I was low and wanted attention. Needless to say, we didn't meet each other's needs.

In a church setting, because of the variety of needs, such conflicts become complex. Some people are desperate for Christian education for their children. Others need the church to offer more recovery groups. Some people find themselves struggling to keep their marriages together; others can't understand why the church isn't doing more for blacks in South Africa. Some want more praise, others more silence, still others more sermon — all in the same worship service! And on it goes.

In most instances, if the church is large enough, people go off and "do their thing," satisfying their needs in one segment of the church. But sometimes churches find themselves having to play one need off of another; they lack the money, people, or time to please everybody. In such cases, I suggest congregations ask themselves:

— Is it possible for one group to defer getting its needs met?

— Is it possible to compromise? Perhaps each group can get some or most of what it needs.

— Are relationships strong enough to weather the possibility of one group not getting their needs met?

In one Illinois church, some leaders felt the worshipers were suffering because of a deteriorating organ. Others felt children were suffering because of poor classroom facilities. In this case, the worshipers got their organ, and the others got the promise of new educational facilities in the future.

This situation also had political and theological dimensions, obviously, which needed to be addressed. But at the heart of the conflict also stood human needs: to worship, to learn. To ignore these legitimate and ongoing needs would have been to ignore one dimension of the problem.

● *Sin.* Although many books on the psychology of conflict omit this category, in my experience, it's a principal cause of church dustups.

I don't have to read the apostle Paul's words on the sinful nature to know that from time to time a voice within me screams that my needs and values are the most important, no matter what! Others can fend for themselves! I readily see how others act selfishly, but I am oblivious to my own selfishness. That attitude only intensifies conflict.

In the case of the California pastor, he clearly saw the judgmental attitude and greed for power in the two men who opposed him. What he didn't see for months, he admits, was his own arrogance and self-righteousness.

The only way to deal with sin, of course, is with repentance. Often that's difficult to do in the middle of a conflict. But if each party can at least recognize the likelihood that their own sin is probably contributing to the conflict, it brings a measure of humility to the process, which helps keep conflict from mushrooming beyond control.

Problems to Solve

Individual shortcomings come from within people, but problems to solve come to the church from "out there." Problems to solve include such things as how much money should be given to missions, whether to buy a photocopy machine, or what stand to take on abortion.

Such problems fall into various categories, each of which suggests a different approach to finding a solution.

● *Issues.* In your garden-variety problem to solve, the disputants have alternatives. They're not stuck with an either/or dilemma but have a variety of choices.

For example, in answer to the question "What shall we do with the $10,000 donated to 'upgrade the church office'?" there are many options: buy a new computer, buy a new photocopier, buy new office furniture for the pastor's study, redo the reception area, and the like.

Further, each option has its own issues: What type of computer, and how large? Which style of furniture? What color paint for the walls?

Basic problem-solving techniques are usually the best way to deal with this form of conflict:

— Clearly define the problem.

— Agree on the problem's definition.

— Explore alternative solutions.

— Develop criteria for selecting one of the alternatives.

— Choose one of the alternatives either by collaboration or by negotiation.

In *a collaborative choice*, both or all of the parties essentially agree. Each party's needs are fully discussed, and solutions are sought that address each party's concerns.

In the example above, $10,000 won't go far enough to get the secretary a new photocopier and the pastor a new office and the church treasurer a new computer. So in a collaborative choice, the secretary gets the photocopier and the pastor new office furnishings. In addition, the pastor trades his new office computer for the treasurer's (the pastor only uses the computer for word processing, and the old computer does that well enough for him).

This is often called a "win-win solution." However, it may be that not all of the parties fully "win" but only that everything possible has been done to arrive at a mutually satisfactory solution.

In *a negotiated choice*, the parties agree on a solution, but there is less commitment to finding solutions that fully satisfy the needs of each party. In negotiation, parties assume they will have to give up one thing to get another.

In the Illinois church that decided for the new organ, the Christian education people were able to get the church board to see the gravity of their needs, but they had to delay for three or four years any improvements in the church school wing.

● *Dichotomies.* In a dichotomy, the possible solutions are limited to two. The choice facing the congregation absolutely excludes the possibility of satisfying both sides of a controversy.

Typical dichotomies churches face include: Should the church change locations? Should the church leave the denomination? Should the organist be replaced?

The answer in each case has to be yes or no. Sometimes it is possible to soften the decision by throwing in something of value to those who "lose," but with truly dichotomous questions, there is a clear winner and loser.

In one church of about 1,800 members, the dichotomy centered around the work of the youth pastor, who was about to be fired. He had made a personal impact on a number of high school youth, but overall attendance was down. Naturally, those parents whose kids were being helped, although small in number, were happy with his work and were stunned to learn that his job was threatened. Other parents could see in the young man only a lack of organization and drive.

The personnel committee had tried to keep the problem from becoming a dichotomy: at first they had called in the youth pastor and told him the concerns most parents were expressing, encouraging him to make changes. But the youth pastor wouldn't or couldn't. He finally had to be let go (with three months severance pay to soften the blow to him and his supporters).

Dichotomies are much more difficult to deal with than issues. Losers can become angry, and they tend not to be committed to the decisions. Sometimes they sabotage agreements or leave a church when they don't get their way.

Actually, anyone who is sensitive to relationships — that includes most people in a church — don't like the tension dichotomies cause. We don't like to see people alienated from one another.

There are two ways, though, to lessen the fallout.

1. You can convince. Leaders can make convincing arguments that cast a new vision of the problem and so entice the disputants along.

Or leaders can convince the opposing group to go along by taking seriously its objections and concerns. When there is a modicum of trust in a church, leaders can help people explore and discuss the issues, and sometimes this process unearths the specific needs of the opposition. Once these needs are expressed openly, the impact of the final decision may be muted: the group may disagree still, but it knows it has been heard.

2. Pay attention to jots and tittles. The pastor of one church was given informal authority to approve infant baptisms. He would interview the couple who wanted their infant baptized, determine if it was appropriate, and then set a date. Later he would get the board's official permission, but that was a mere formality.

One time, however, a young couple who didn't attend church and were merely living together asked him if he would baptize their child. The pastor balked, but the man was on the church rolls as a member; according to church law, he had the right to have his child baptized.

The pastor knew, however, that the final decision for baptisms rested in the hands of the board — only it could refuse the man his right. Rather than exerting his informal prerogatives, the pastor decided to do everything according to the church constitution.

He took the decision to the board, explained the facts, made no recommendation, and asked for the board's decision. The board voted against the baptism, and the pastor relayed their decision to the man and his girl friend.

The couple was not pleased, but they couldn't fault the pastor or church for anything other than disagreeing with them. If you have to make a decision and you can't get full agreement, at least proceed according to civil and church law.

● *Value Differences.* Value differences are not seen as often in churches as are issues and dichotomies, because congregations are expert at making sure that these types of problems do not come to the fore. Congregations instinctively know that a values conflict is tortuous to work through and the likelihood of finding agreement low.

A few church members, for example, might object to any

divorced person being in leadership positions; others believe that forgiveness of divorce extends to letting people lead the congregation. Or some members might believe that a minimum of 10 percent of the church's budget should be designated for overseas missions; others believe local missions should be the first priority.

It's not easy for people to dispute about values. First, people's identities rest on their deeply held values; so they do not change easily.

Also, in churches especially, people are admonished to maintain their values, to refuse to compromise what they hold dear; we regularly hold up for admiration the great martyrs of the faith who remained true to the faith.

So with values, a great deal is at stake. If values come up, people are not inclined to say, "I am open to listen to your argument; I am ready to change my mind if necessary." People are more interested in getting their way because their way is "right."

When faced with value differences, the church has a few options:

1. Reframe the problem. One church was struggling to decide whether people should be allowed to speak in tongues in worship. The issue distressed the church's leaders because the choices were virtually dichotomous, and they didn't want to split the church over the issue.

A third party, however, tried to help the situation by pointing out that people in the church had become alienated from one another; they were no longer communicating as they had in the past. This group managed to change the issue from speaking in tongues to how people should communicate better.

You can also reframe the issue by helping people explore their areas of agreement: their common commitment to Jesus as Lord, their love for the church, their deep respect for the contributions made by their opponents. Then, looking at what holds them together, they can work more irenically on the disagreement.

Frankly, reframing the issue doesn't really deal with the issue. If the issue is not that important, reframing works. But if the issue is a major concern to people, reframing can be short-lived strategy. The problem will present itself again, perhaps in a more vehement form, because the problem has lingered, perhaps festered, without resolution.

2. Partition. To partition means to ensure that the disputing parties do not share the same space at the same time (at least at certain critical times). In the case of the controversy over appropriate behavior in worship, those more charismatic in worship would meet at one hour and those less demonstrative would meet at another.

I have used this technique with budgets as well as programs. A congregation in Iowa had a dispute over how to spend their missions money. One group felt all the church's mission money should go to the denomination's missions, mostly hospitals, self-help projects, and education. Another group felt strongly that this money should be used primarily for evangelism.

Since they couldn't come to agreement, we decided that the church should have two missions committees, each with an equal share of the outreach monies of the church, each deciding how it would spend its share of the money. Neither party, however, was fully happy with this "solution," but it was better than any other alternative they could think of at the time.

3. Agree not to deal with the issue. Sometimes not making any decision is actually the best decision. As long as the church acknowledges this openly, it's an honest way to deal with values differences.

One church had for fifteen years shared the facilities of another congregation. In that time, about half the congregation became convinced that this was the church's unique identity: a congregation that was a good steward of its resources, a church that was people, not buildings.

The other half of the congregation pined away for a building. They believed the church would go nowhere unless it had its own physical identity.

When a new pastor came to the church, he kept getting different messages about which way to lead the church. He finally organized a goal-setting process in which this issue was discussed — and then dropped. People realized that there was no consensus on the issue, and so they thought it best to leave things the way they were for the time being.

4. Get a "divorce." If all of your efforts to come to agreement have failed, and the issue is deeply held values, then one group may simply have to leave. It's a solution that is terribly costly, but sometimes it's better for everyone concerned.

The two men who disputed with the California pastor eventually left the church. When they did, everyone breathed a sigh of relief. The issues between them and the pastor were never solved, but the church was able to get back to ministry, and the two men and their families were able to find a church home where they could better serve.

Behavioral Patterns

Students of family life have noted that behaviors of family members are often practiced apart from the conscious decisions of individuals themselves. Divorce, substance abuse, and suicide are notable examples of repetitive patterns that move in families from one generation to the next.

Social behavioral patterns are often subtle. For example, when I was on the debate team in high school, there was an unwritten rule in our debating club, and certainly in formal debates themselves, that personal attack and rigorous challenge of everything the other said and did was fair game. So I found myself often, in the context of the debate team, challenging, attacking, putting others down with relish and abandon. But I certainly never acted that way at home or in other social contexts.

Likewise, each church has unwritten rules about how it goes about disagreeing. In one church, every squabble is immediately taken to the pastor for his adjudication. In another church, disputes are publicly avoided and handled by gossip. But however the dispute is handled, it is not necessarily handled consciously. People have learned over the years how to handle congregational conflict, and they may not even be able to articulate exactly what they do.

But often, especially when the pattern of behavior remains

unexamined, it damages terribly a church's life.

I worked with a congregation that called itself a "Matthew 18 church." They said they managed conflict by following the guidelines of Jesus as laid out in Matthew 18. Those guidelines spell out a process whereby a person who has sinned is confronted first by an individual, and if the "sinner" remains unconvinced, then by individuals not involved in the dispute, and if still not convinced, then by the entire congregation.

Unfortunately, this "Matthew 18 church" simply used this method to vent anger at one another. An angry member would seek out a person who annoyed him, berate the person for his rude and thoughtless conduct, and then escape from further conversation. People didn't seek to understand one another, let alone compromise. It was simply hit and run.

This behavior didn't result merely from people's anger or frustration or personality conflicts. A large part of the problem was "institutional" — this was the way the church had handled conflict for years. No one knew how to do it any differently.

Helping a congregation move beyond their usual patterns is difficult at best. It calls for two courses of action.

1. Notice the behavior. The people need to see what they're doing and how it's destructive to the church.

Usually groups need help from someone outside their institution to figure out what's going on. The outsider will notice patterns to which an insider is blind.

2. Learn new behaviors. Once a congregation is aware of how it normally handles conflict, it's less likely to continue the pattern. The game is up; people know what's coming next; they also know that it's an unproductive way to proceed.

Still, learning new behaviors is not easy. I remember when I first learned about active listening (responding to people with words and posture to assure them of my interest), I was thrilled. Immediately, I knew exactly what I was supposed to do, but actually doing it was terribly awkward at first. I needed a good deal of practice, with feedback from a person with a practiced eye, to develop sufficient skill.

If a congregation has learned to deal with disagreement by gossip or attack or whatever, it's going to take some preaching, teaching, and perhaps seminars by outsiders to show people new ways of relating. And sometimes it takes a gentle but direct confrontation of people who continue the old ways.

One pastor was becoming frustrated with the way his congregation dealt with him about disagreements: people would talk behind his back, and he would have to fish and fish to discover the substance of people's concerns.

So he diplomatically pointed out this behavior in newsletters and in sermons, explaining how much energy and time this behavior wasted, and how many hurt feelings it could engender. He also told his people that if they had a problem with the church, rather than gossiping about it, they should simply write him a note or tell him directly. He admitted that he might not be able to deal with their complaint satisfactorily, but at least he would be aware of what people were thinking, and that would help him be a more sensitive pastor overall.

Well, the pattern continued, especially by three or four key men in the church. Then one day, the pastor happened to run into one of these men while making a hospital call. He asked the man, thirty years his senior, to have a cup of coffee with him.

After a few pleasant amenities, the pastor came to the point, "Stan, I understand you've not been happy with the change in the order of worship."

Stan was silent.

"And I know you've been talking to John and Jack about your complaints."

Stan squirmed.

"I'm going to be straight with you, Stan." The pastor leaned forward and looked Stan directly in the eye. "I would be helped and the church would be helped if, when you've got a problem with the way I'm doing something, you come to me directly. Complaining to others about my decisions has got to stop. It undermines my ministry and demoralizes the church."

Stan mumbled a weak agreement, and soon after he became a strong, albeit not uncritical, supporter of the pastor. The habit of congregational gossip had been dealt a severe blow.

Church conflict makes a church feel as if it's being swept along by a raging flood. And often it is that way. But if the church can discover the various and sundry tributaries that feed into the conflict, they can turn flood waters that destroy into a river that gently but powerfully moves them downstream.

Pastors know that church conflict is coming. Knowing when it's apt to come is a different matter and one that pastors are wise to be alert to.

— Speed Leas

CHAPTER EIGHT

The Ten Most Predictable Times of Conflict

P astors have learned not to be discouraged the week after Christmas or the week after Easter. Those Sundays are traditionally the lowest in attendance. Coming as they do immediately after high points in the church year, the unprepared pastor sets himself up for despair if he doesn't recognize the pattern.

In the same way, pastors are better prepared for church conflict if they know when it's more likely to come. Certainly, pastors know *that* church conflict is coming — it has been part of the church since day one. Knowing *when* it's apt to come is a different matter and one that pastors are wise to be alert to.

"For everything there is a season," intoned the author of Ecclesiastes. He didn't mention it in his list, but he could have included church conflict. In my work with churches, I seem to get more calls for help during ten particular times in a congregation's life.

1. Easter

During Lent and just after Easter the number of calls for help received by the Alban Institute rises substantially: up 28 percent over the normal number of calls per month.

Easter is usually the busiest time of year — even outdoing Advent and Christmas. Usually during Lent, a church offers more programs and worship services, and attendance is up. All that creates more stress and tension, and any underlying or submerged conflicts more easily surface.

In addition, when Easter arrives, church leaders realize that there are only a couple of months, before the summer slow-down, to take care of problems that have developed in the program year.

Perhaps the youth sponsors have been sporadic in their efforts with the high school group. The associate pastor doesn't want to ignore this problem until the fall — otherwise he may end up letting it go another year. Better to nip it in the bud and start the next year's program in a fresh way.

So he asks another couple to become youth sponsors and encourages the present sponsors to retire when summer comes.

The present sponsors are hurt, and use the occasion to complain about the work of the associate, about which they've not been happy for some time. Pretty soon, the problem of high school sponsors becomes the entire church's problem — another Eastertide conflict.

2. Stewardship Campaigns/Budget Time

In November and December of each year, I receive several calls from pastors and/or lay leaders about what they discovered during their annual stewardship campaign: when the church callers spoke with the members of the congregation about their pledges, they not only received less money than was expected, they also learned that members were unhappy. The every-member canvass has uncovered some deeper problems in the church, and the problems may have little to do with money.

In a Michigan congregation, giving had dropped off markedly, and the position of some staff members was in jeopardy. So the board decided to call on all of the members of the church to request their financial support. They trained a cadre of leaders to visit every member: they wanted to listen to each member's hopes and concerns for the church and then tell them what the church was doing, inviting them to increase their pledges.

When they asked for volunteers to make the calls, few people at first responded. When they finally did get enough callers and made the calls, the board was surprised at the response: the callers heard a great deal of dissatisfaction from the members — about the pastor's preaching, the staff's sloppy work in religious education, and the general dreariness of the worship services.

The board had been unaware of members' feelings because, in general, church members usually did not speak directly to one another, let alone the board, about their dissatisfaction with the church. The every-member canvass provided a channel for their complaints.

3. Addition of New Staff

The most frequent type of conflict in congregations is between the pastor and key leaders in the church. This is particularly true when a new pastoral staff member is called.

New staff means not only changes in relationships and procedures but also changes in directions and priorities.

I worked with one congregation that had two interim pastors during its two-year search for a pastor. The interims were passive leaders, who seldom interfered with the leadership of the church. As a result, eight laypeople emerged to carry the church through the interim.

These eight people were delighted when the new pastor arrived — at last they wouldn't have to spend so much time at the church; they would get a rest as somebody else handled all the details.

But when the new pastor started to handle the details, the eight leaders found themselves sorely disappointed. The pastor made decisions all right, but differently than they would have. What was worse, he tended to listen to the views of others more than he did theirs!

4. Change in Leadership Style

In another congregation, the pastor was introverted — quiet, reserved, bookish, but thoughtful and caring. The problem was he followed a highly extroverted pastor, who loved being with people, in the church and in the community.

Members felt awkward having to take the initiative in conversation with the new pastor, and they became impatient for the new pastor to warm up to them. In fact, the pace of his interaction was simply different than what they were used to, and that took some getting used to.

When a congregation hires, either deliberately or by mistake, a pastor whose leadership style differs from his predecessor, conflict is a near certainty.

Leadership problems are often "followership" problems. For a leader to lead effectively, people must follow effectively — people must actively cooperate with the pastor's style of leadership.

For example, some families experience more turmoil when their children become teenagers. It's not that the parents have changed, but the children, now teenagers, have. They no longer want to follow the style of leadership the parents have been exerting for years. Leadership is only as effective as the followers.

Often congregations will choose a new pastor with the express intent of picking someone who offers a style of leadership different than the previous pastor — let's say the last pastor was an authoritative leader and the new pastor participatory (a not unusual occurrence in congregations).

In this scenario, things may go well until there is a congregational crisis or major decision. Then people become anxious, and they revert to old patterns of behavior — and they expect others, like the pastor, to follow suit. They want the pastor suddenly to become decisive and bold. At this point, everyone becomes confused.

5. The Pastor's Vacation

While the pastor of one Presbyterian congregation was away on his honeymoon, the Session (the church board) met to discuss his leadership. They decided it was serious enough to phone him in the middle of his honeymoon; they told him a delegation was being sent to the presbytery to ask help from the committee on ministry.

Ouch!

Is this typical? No. But if serious problems are festering in a church, it's not surprising that the dissatisfied group will gather to discuss them while the pastor is away.

Also, some churches depend unduly on their pastor, so that when he or she does take a vacation, the people subconsciously panic. One group begins squabbling with another, or the associate says something offensive from the pulpit ("If you're not giving a tithe to this church, you're not fully committed to Christ!") and people react. Before long, someone feels compelled to phone the vacationing pastor to tell him things are falling apart.

6. Changes in the Pastor's Family

Often changes in a pastor's family, even for the better, will cause conflict in the congregation.

One pastor for years devoted his primary energy and attention, to the congregation. The congregation got used to his seventy- and eighty-hour weeks.

When the pastor's daughter reached her teens, he and his daughter began quarreling more. She began to get into trouble at school. The pastor was concerned.

So he started to spend a great deal more time at home, and he began attending a weekly therapy session with his wife and daughter.

Well, the church started feeling neglected. Even though the pastor still put in some fifty hours a week, the congregation complained about his flagging interest in the church.

7. Introduction of Baby Boomers into the Church

Over the last ten years, a new generation of churchgoers has begun to participate in congregational life. These so-called "baby boomers" tend to be more liberal than previous generations, and they live significantly different lifestyles: typically both parents work full time, they have little free time, they hold only short-term commitments, they tend only to support programs that meet their needs, and they tend to be more forthright and outspoken.

This has presented many a problem to churches. Women's groups find it difficult to attract working women; program planners are annoyed by the baby boomers' unwillingness to make long-term commitments; committees are aggravated by baby boomers' commitment to excellence, especially when it comes to programs and facilities for children, because excellence is a lot of trouble!

All this can be aggravating to the older generation.

8. The Completion of a New Building

When the Alban Institute researched pastoral firings, it discovered that after the completion of a new building, clergy were vulnerable to firing. Several factors are involved:

The leadership (including the pastor's) has centered on a focused and specific task. Once completed, a new kind of leadership is required — usually leadership focused on program.

If the transition is not made, the church, which had experienced itself as successful, now feels it's drifting. It wants the kind of energy and focus it had during the building project. Unless it finds a new focus, the frustration gets directed into a conflict.

9. Loss of Church Membership

Conflict is more likely when a church endures significant drops in membership. Membership is a scarce resource for many congregations; as resources — money or people — dwindle, tension increases.

Members of declining congregations often pin the blame for their problems on a person or group, even though the people they blame may have done little if anything to contribute to the difficulty.

In upstate New York, a downtown parish had suffered a slow, regular, and significant decrease in attendance for ten years. The pastor, who had been with the church for fifteen years, knew that part of the decline was due to urban renewal, which had removed much of the housing near the church. In addition, two new congregations of the same denomination had been started not far away in the suburbs.

Still, he was convinced that the *real* reason the church had been losing members was three older women of the congregation: They had controlled the church for twenty years. They resisted everything he tried. They were hostile and forbidding. They intimidated anyone who wanted to try something new, whether it was a new church school class, a program for the homeless, or innovations in worship.

While many of the members agreed that the problem was this formidable troika, an equally large group thought the problem lay with the pastor: he didn't pay enough attention to the older members, he didn't call on the members frequently enough, and he was too involved in controversial social issues about the poor.

Which group was "right"? Both and neither. But the pain of membership loss was so great, each felt the need to blame someone.

I pointed out to both sides that although the women and the pastor could each improve how they worked in the church, the membership problems were largely caused by factors beyond the control of any individual or group. Consequently, I encouraged them to identify ways they might strengthen their church's work in their community and discouraged their attempts to improve each other.

10. Increase in Church Membership

On the other hand, an increase in church membership can also trigger conflict, because as congregations grow, their personalities change. People happy with the old personality usually don't like the new personality that emerges.

As do others, I classify congregations into four sizes: family, pastoral, program, and corporate.

● *Family size.* These congregations average less than fifty on Sunday morning. They tend to be single-cell organizations with only one dominant leader — usually not the pastor, rather a long-term and active member of the congregation. Family-size congregations tend to look to the past, to what has or has not worked, to guide their decisions.

● *Pastoral size.* These churches average 50 to 150 people on Sunday morning. They have several cells, or primary groups. These cells tend to relate to each other through the pastor.

The pastor links the congregation. Usually it is the pastor who calls on newcomers and acquaints them with others in the congregation. He orients them to congregational life and helps them find a place to land — a committee, a Bible study, the choir. Furthermore, the pastor is about the only person who attends every church function.

The pastor, then, wields more authority in a pastoral-size congregation than in the family-size church. People look to the pastor for information and advice.

Planning in pastoral-size congregations is still determined by what has happened in the past, although not as much as in the family-size congregation.

As a church moves into the pastoral-size category, the matriarch or patriarch will lose his or her power to the pastor, and this transition will not be easy.

Also, as the congregation swells, it begins functioning in distinct groups. Those who formerly liked the unified, family feel of the church are likely to complain.

● *Program size.* These congregations have from 150 to 350 on

Sunday morning. Since duties exceed the physical capabilities of a single pastor, the church hires other staff and delegates more work to boards and committees.

Not everyone in the congregation works directly with the senior pastor, but some relate to the music personnel, others to the Christian education director, and others still to the associate pastor. Thus, to some the congregation feels like an "organization" rather than a church.

Exigencies often determine planning. Members get in trouble with one another for scheduling two events in the same room on the same day, or attempting to take the young people on a weekend retreat on the Sunday of the all-church picnic. Planning worship is more complex, since the interests of the music personnel, the preacher, and the worship committee all have to be coordinated.

(Actually, congregations with more than 150 on Sunday morning can function like a pastoral-size church. Such a church usually has few committees and offers few programs. The church essentially revolves around the Sunday morning worship service.)

The shift from a pastoral-size congregation to a program-size congregation is likely to be more disquieting still. The changes will be more visible, thus threatening to more people.

For example, changing from one worship service to two will likely be the most disturbing change for the church: "The church will no longer be unified." "We won't be able to see our friends if they attend another service."

Usually congregations restructure their boards when they move from pastoral- to program-size congregations. The governing board no longer works as closely with all aspects of the congregation's life. Some committees report less and some not at all to the governing board, and consequently many people feel increasingly alienated from church leadership.

The pastor restructures his schedule as well. He or she can no longer visit everyone who is sick and shut in and meet with every committee. That is felt as a real loss to everyone, including the pastor.

• *Corporate size.* These congregations, with more than 350

people on Sunday morning, are even more hierarchically organized than program-size churches. The pastor now relates only to program staff, certainly not all staff. Often the pastor focuses more on his unique ministry (usually preaching), and others have the administrative and program responsibilities.

Often cadres, groups, special ministries, or even pastoral-size churches emerge within the corporate-size congregation. The pastor becomes a symbol who holds the entire congregation together.

Planning now is more complex, but in addition to responding to the needs of the moment, corporate-size churches have the time and staff to base their decisions on future contingencies.

Many of the same tensions experienced in the previous size change are felt here as well.

What can be done to better deal with these predictable times of conflict?

Knowing the stages of grief helps; after all, nearly all of these occasions have something to do with letting go of something past.

Also, knowing that conflict and stress, at low levels anyway, are helpful for congregations, helps reduce some of the tension brought on by these transitions.

But in any event, just knowing what may come helps.

A football receiver often knows he's going to be hit immediately after he makes a catch. Knowing that doesn't lessen the impact of the hit, but it does help him to hold on to the ball and sometimes even maintain his balance, elude the tackler, and gain some extra ground.

Likewise with pastors: if they know when the church is likely to be hit, they'll more likely be able to turn up field for a few extra yards.

Part 4
Special Cases

Ultimately, in the restoration process, you've got to make a judgment call. Because discernment is so difficult, a group needs to be involved — no individual is capable of seeing the whole picture.

— Edward Dobson

CHAPTER NINE

Restoring a Fallen Colleague

The sanctuary of Temple Baptist Church near Detroit is an imposing and intimidating structure. Built in the late 1960s, it seats 4,000 people. The church has a rich tradition in the independent Baptist movement, at the forefront of the evangelism, Sunday school, and church growth movements of the twentieth century.

I had spoken there many times before on happier occasions. But on this Sunday as I sat on the platform, it was different. I tried to sing the hymns, but I cried. I tried to concentrate on the special music, but my attention was riveted on the family in the first row.

They were clinging to each other as if afraid to let go. They looked out of place, even though they had been in the church for years.

I tried to smile at them, and they tried to smile back. But it was obvious to both of us that there was little to smile about.

Many in the choir had tears in their eyes. It was like a funeral service: everyone putting on the best front possible, yet feeling that at any moment the emotions could come unglued.

It might have been easier had I not been so close to the family in the front row. Truman Dollar was a mentor and a friend. When I was considering leaving Thomas Road Baptist Church in Lynchburg, Virginia, it was Truman who counseled me nearly every day. When I moved to Grand Rapids and needed advice in making decisions as a pastor, I turned to him.

Looking at him now from the pulpit, I could not believe he was about to resign as pastor. It all seemed so unreal.

The events of the last week flooded my mind.

The Unwelcome News

On the previous Monday, the phone rang. I answered, and in his resonant voice, Jerry Falwell, the man I'd worked with for almost fifteen years, said, "What are you doing?"

"Nothing," I replied. "I had to answer the phone." We laughed.

Jerry quickly got serious.

"Have you heard about Truman's situation?" Without waiting for an answer, he continued, "I just talked to Curt Wilson, the chairman of the Temple Baptist deacon board. Truman has had some problems and is going to resign. They wanted me to come and help, but my visibility would only hurt the situation. Since you've helped in these kinds of situations before, I suggested that he call you." He briefly described some of the problems and assured me of his prayer and support.

"Call me if you need any help," he said.

Shortly after I hung up the phone, it rang again.

"Dr. Dobson," the voice said, "Dr. Jerry Falwell suggested I call you to see if you could help us." Curt Wilson and I spent almost an hour on the phone.

He explained that two years ago, Truman's 15-year-old son had overheard him talking to a woman from their former church. The conversation contained inappropriate sexual content. The son, not knowing what to do, told the youth pastor what he had heard, who in turn confronted Truman.

Truman admitted he had spoken inappropriately, asked forgiveness, and the matter seemed settled.

Now, two years later, that episode resurfaced, and the entire deacon board had been informed. After a lengthy and stormy meeting, the deacons concluded they should ask for Truman's resignation.

"The announcement will be made this coming Sunday," Curt said. "Would you be willing to preach on Sunday morning and evening, and meet with our deacons to begin sorting through the specific steps that need to be taken?"

"First of all, I would need to consult our board for their advice and wisdom," I said. "I haven't been here that long, and I made an agreement to submit to their authority; I would not want to do something so dramatic without their complete support." I made arrangements for an emergency board meeting the next day at noon.

I didn't sleep much that night. I was shocked, disappointed, and hurt. I knew this would be a long and difficult week. I wasn't sure what our board would think. I wasn't even sure I was capable of giving advice or leadership in this complex situation. I did decide, however, that I would not walk away from Truman. He had been my friend, was still my friend, and would always be my friend. Whether or not I got officially involved in the situation, I would still stand by his side.

The next day at the emergency board meeting, almost everyone was there. While a few kidded and laughed before the meeting, everyone could tell something serious was about to happen. I'm sure some of them thought perhaps I was in trouble.

After I recounted my conversation with Curt Wilson and Jerry Falwell, the board unanimously encouraged me to go to Temple, work with their deacon board, and preach for them on Sunday.

But they also felt that the pressure of this situation should not be faced alone. They promised to pray for my ministry at Temple, and they appointed three men to go with me as a source of encouragement, strength, wisdom, and support.

In retrospect, I am deeply grateful that these men went with me. Ken Ellis, the youngest member, is a licensed psychologist and has keen insight into human behavior. Adrian VanWyk, the elder statesman of the group, is one of the pastors at our church and had been through similar church situations before. Philip Nymeyer is a no-nonsense, get-to-the-bottom-line businessman. I knew that in a tense situation, these men could get to the fundamental issues quickly.

On Wednesday, I traveled alone to Detroit to meet with Curt Wilson, some of the staff, and the Dollar family. It was a long drive. I had several hours for reflection. I thought about the many times that Truman and I had talked together on the telephone. I thought about the time we were together in California when he was struggling with whether to leave his former church in Kansas City and move to Detroit. I remember his pain as he sought to do what God wanted.

I thought about the time we were together at a conference with sixty other fundamentalist preachers. I delivered a lecture on the differences between liberals, evangelicals, and fundamentalists. I remember his willingness to be used as my illustration of a not-quite-true fundamentalist because he wore a gold chain around his neck. People laughed and clapped. I also remembered jogging with Truman the next day.

I recalled the times he had come to Lynchburg. As columnists for *Fundamentalist Journal*, we would often read our material to one another over the phone and suggest changes to each other. We had developed a kinship over the years, and I was afraid our relationship was about to change forever.

Talking with Truman

When I pulled into his driveway, I noticed a FOR SALE sign in front of the house. When I walked in the house, Truman and Donna embraced me, and we stood together and cried. As we talked, Donna made it clear she was completely supportive of her husband.

"I'm determined to stand with him — whatever happens," she said.

The rest of the family was there, and it was a house filled with activity. Truman and I excused ourselves and went to the basement, a large room, carpeted and paneled, empty except for a desk and a couple of folding chairs in one corner. The family had often hosted large groups of church members there. And there we sat, and through the tears he poured out his story to me.

He talked about how hard the move from Kansas City to Detroit had been on his family — how they had to leave home and friends.

He told about the increasing pressure of the ministry, about coming from a church he'd built for over twenty years into a church that had a lot of problems and was in decline, a church that wasn't overly receptive to him.

He mentioned how the decision to admit blacks into membership had cost the church several families. The recent discussion about relocating the church was even more volatile. And Truman was the target of most of the anger.

During this period, he had been talking to a couple who were lifelong friends. Sometimes when the husband wasn't home, Truman would talk to the wife. During those conversations, Truman began sharing the pressures and discouragement he was feeling.

Later Truman said, "Looking back, that was a fatal mistake. There were other people who could have listened. I said things that were inappropriate and wrong. I'm embarrassed and ashamed of what I said. I was neither unfaithful physically nor were we ever together. But with my suggestive language, I was clearly in sin. I still find it hard to talk about what I said to her."

It was during one of those conversations that his teenage son picked up another extension and listened in. He was shocked by what he heard.

Shortly thereafter, his son went on a youth retreat. He talked privately to the youth pastor about what he had heard his dad say. When they came back from the retreat, the son and the youth pastor confronted Truman. He reluctantly admitted he had said those things.

"This kind of language and conversation is completely out of character for me," said Truman. "I asked their forgiveness and promised to stop any further conversations with this woman."

They agreed that no one else needed to know about this.

But the secret between Truman and the youth pastor created intense pressure. Their relationship began to deteriorate.

"When the youth pastor would do something poorly and I would talk to him about it, he would say, 'Well, I guess I'm not the only person who has messed up.' As his performance slipped, I thought about firing him, but it was clear, at least to me, that he was holding our secret over my head. He repeatedly threatened me, and I knew he could go public.

"In retrospect," said Truman, "I should have gone to the deacon board right then, told them what was happening to me, and asked for their help. They probably would have put me on a leave of absence, gotten me some help, and nursed me back to health."

In time, however, the youth pastor confided in some other staff members. The church had been incurring excessive long-distance telephone charges, so Truman installed a device to log the numbers of all calls placed. Reviewing the log one month, one of those church staff members noted the number of the woman who had been involved in the inappropriate conversations had been called from Truman's line. Assuming the conversations had resumed, he told the whole story to some others.

One Sunday, right after the morning service, the staff members confronted Truman in his office with their accusations and documentation.

"What in fact had happened," said Truman, "is that the woman's husband had called when I was out. I returned the call and talked to him. I didn't consider that a recurrence. I tried to present my side of things, but the staff members insisted the incident had not been handled properly two years before, and now they wanted my immediate resignation.

"It didn't take me long to discover that this confrontation involved more than a discussion of purity. It was a well-planned revolution, a palace coup. If I didn't resign, they said, they would make the matter public.

"I didn't bother to defend myself. I was humiliated and helpless. All of a sudden, something I thought had been taken care of was exposed."

Truman later admitted to me that he was traumatized that afternoon, not thinking or acting logically after the painful confrontation by several staff members: "I was left alone in my office for a few minutes. My mind played tricks on me. I thought that perhaps the damage done to my family and the church would be minimized if I were not alive.

"My youngest son's 30-30 deer rifle was in my office; a staff member had recently cleaned it for me. I took a soft-nosed shell from a case and nervously shoved it into the chamber. For a fleeting moment I thought the easiest thing would be to end it all."

Fortunately, Truman's wife and secretary arrived about that time, and he was not left alone again. He didn't tell his wife.

"I realize how self-centered this would have been," he later told me. "I was thinking only of myself. It was also a denial of everything I had ever preached about accountability, about God caring and being in control." (He was so embarrassed that only after three years was he able to admit publicly the incident.)

That night, Truman and Donna walked slowly out of the church study toward the two flights of stairs that would lead them to the parking lot. It had been a long afternoon. From the nearby auditorium of historic Temple Baptist Church in Detroit, they could hear the congregation singing hymns they had known all of their lives. The Sunday evening service had begun.

"It was the first time in thirty years that for a reason other than illness we had missed a Sunday evening service," he said. "It seemed strange not to be there. I was officially still the pastor, but in my heart I knew that would change quickly — everything would change quickly. We were in great pain."

They thought about the congregation, which was also in pain that night. The church was not told why Truman was not in the pulpit. The congregation knew nothing of the events that transpired that afternoon. They would not learn until the next Sunday.

That night Truman and Donna just wanted to disappear — so they spent that night alone: "We did not want to meet or talk to anyone. Donna and I were both numb, silent, overwhelmed with the events of the afternoon. Our whole world had just caved in. We felt abandoned by both God and man. We were both stunned. Thirty years of ministry gone — no job, no security, no future."

Still, in a curious way, Truman was relieved that he would now be forced to deal with his sin: "My repentance had been private but incomplete. Now I could deal with it thoroughly and publicly."

He recognized that he needed to make restitution to people whom he had injured with his actions, and although restoration was not going to be easy, he was determined to begin the process: "There's never a convenient time to interrupt life and deal with burdensome personal problems," he later said, "but that day's events forced me to deal with them. It's clear that a sovereign God determined the time of my restoration in his own wisdom, but it was not all that obvious then. Still, I resolved then and there to begin to rebuild my broken life."

About that night he also told me: "I know that I was not thinking clearly, but that night I developed a strange sense of peace, and there was almost no anxiety."

Two days before I had my talk with Truman, he had begun the task of informing people whom he needed to tell personally. It was much like informing the members of the family when a death has occurred, he said.

At 2 p.m. that day, he called his daughter Sonya and his son Tim, both of whom live in Kansas City with their spouses. By 5:30 that afternoon, both of them were on a plane to Detroit to join

Truman and Donna. They stayed the entire week, and all the family members were by his side on the platform the next Sunday when he publicly resigned.

Truman later told me that during that week, he became increasingly aware of the historical significance of what was occurring: "I knew each word would be recorded and every scratch of paper saved in the archives of the church. I remembered the hours I spent reading some of those decade-old records of bitter conflict. Now, my own name was to appear and the record would not be good. I could not voice how regretful I was at how future generations would likely judge me."

I realized other factors were at work in all this. It suddenly occurred to me that every time I'd talked to Truman in the last year or so, he'd mentioned how tired he was, how hard he was working, how difficult the situation was, how spiritually drained he felt. I suspected that he saw resignation as at least some ray of hope that *I can get off this treadmill and out of this rat race.*

After our conversation that afternoon, Truman wanted to get out of the house and away from the telephone. So Truman, his two sons, and I played an afternoon of golf. The sun was shining; the course was beautiful. For a few temporary moments, everything was normal again. Tim talked about his law practice. Devon talked about his girlfriends. I talked about Calvary Church. Truman talked about golf.

All too quickly the game ended, and we rode back to Truman's house. We walked past the FOR SALE sign and back into the harsh reality of an uncertain future.

I returned to Grand Rapids.

Identifying My Goals in the Process

I met my traveling companions at 2 P.M. in the parking lot of Calvary Church the next Saturday. We packed our stuff in the back of a Jeep Cherokee and made the trip from Grand Rapids to Detroit. I updated the men on my conversations with Truman, Curt, and others.

Pastor VanWyk recounted in detail his experience with a similar situation many years ago. He told us about the long-term consequences of that incident in the people's lives and how the church had become divided over the issue. Some people wanted to forgive the pastor and accept him as if nothing had happened. Others wanted to defrock him forever. Others didn't know what to do. Pastor VanWyk had served as a moderator, and as a result, much of the anger in the church had been directed toward him.

I was beginning to sense that there was no simple, predictable strategy with which to respond to this situation. The damage had been done, and the best that we could do was exercise some sort of damage control.

But as we drove, the role I would need to play began coming into focus. I identified four goals. I vowed to try

1. To ensure that they treated Truman with dignity. Even if he had done wrong, it wasn't right to stomp on him.

2. To help the church work through the shock and the swirling emotions, and to help them see that there was hope beyond this, that this was not the end of effective ministry at Temple.

3. To communicate a biblical perspective. The key in all of this was to respond not according to what they felt but according to the principles of Scripture. I knew that some people in the church were delighted Truman messed up; they didn't like him to begin with. The whole church, and especially these people, needed to accept the biblical command to forgive.

4. To discourage the church from making hasty decisions. While some people would want Truman's head on a platter, others would insist he hadn't done anything seriously wrong. Some would want him skinned alive; others would want to vote him back in as pastor. My goal was to help prevent the church from splitting.

The Divisive Decision

We checked into the Holiday Inn and went to dinner. Curt Wilson joined us, and we talked about the deacons meeting to be held that evening. We then rode together to the church. Everyone was there, including the staff member who had confronted Truman several years before and the staff members and deacon who had confronted him the previous week, bringing the issue to the full deacon board.

I looked around the room. I felt sorry for the staff and deacons. They had lost their leader. They seemed unsure of what to do.

The first couple of hours of the meeting were spent recounting the details of the situation and the steps that had been taken so far in dealing with it. It quickly became clear that the group was significantly divided. Everyone felt that Truman had done wrong. However, some felt that the actions of those who accused Truman were just as wrong as what Truman had done.

Some tense charges and countercharges were exchanged:

"It's obvious that some leaders in this church are willing to sweep sin under the rug, to forsake their integrity to prevent embarrassment."

"It looks to me as though some people on staff here are trying to use this unfortunate episode to further their own careers. If anyone should come under church discipline, it's the staff!"

"This thing is two years old, and there hasn't been a recurrence of the questionable behavior. Truman should stay on as pastor."

"When such a serious sin is committed, spiritual leadership is forfeited!"

We reached an impasse. The three men from our church were sitting in the back, and I could see them bowed in prayer. I knew God was our only hope for bringing harmony to the group.

"Listen," I said. "The real issue here is not whether we like the way things were handled. The issue is that we have a pastor who's resigned, and we need to address that issue."

I suggested that we pray, and I insisted that we all get on our knees.

I began, not knowing what I would say. It was one of the longest prayers I have ever uttered in a public meeting. I prayed for those in leadership, for the Dollar family, and for the church. Then I broke down and began sobbing. I asked God to protect each of us from making these same kind of mistakes. I told God I didn't want ever to embarrass his name. I didn't want to let down the church that called me as its pastor. I didn't want to hurt my family. By the time I was through praying almost everyone in the room was weeping.

Then we took a break. When we came back, we began dealing with how we were going to face tomorrow. I sensed a different spirit at that point. Instead of *Where should we attach the blame?* the question became *How do we proceed from here?* Amid the tension, we all seemed to realize that if we were to sit in a position of authority and decision making, we needed to be humble before the Lord.

We also realized that regardless of how serious we each thought Truman's blunder or how meaningful we judged his repentance, we knew he couldn't stay on as pastor — the anger and confusion of so many members made continuing untenable. So we discussed Truman's resignation and what needed to happen.

After some disagreement, we finally concluded that Truman should personally read the statement to the church. Some, especially on the staff, felt it should be read for him, that Truman shouldn't even be there. They wanted him just to disappear.

I responded, "If you handle it that way, it will appear to the congregation that he got railroaded. And if that's the perception, they'll railroad every staff member out of here. Unless people can see that Truman is convinced this is the right thing to do, the church will split. Our only chance to minimize the damage is for him to be there and allow people to see him, to see his family, to hear him confess his wrong. And they need opportunity afterward to say good-bye."

The group also agreed that Curt and I should meet with Truman to discuss the resignation and the events of the next day. We concluded that the statement should be honest about the reason for his resignation, although not explicit. We decided he should simply say he'd had "inappropriate conversations" with a woman.

We knew that what he read and how he read it would have a profound impact on how the congregation would respond. Indeed, the statement would serve as a document people would repeatedly refer to. In fact, one of the later sources of conflict was over the fact that the word *sin* was not used. In retrospect, perhaps it should have been, although those angry at Truman would probably have found other things to criticize.

We discussed how the resignation should be handled publicly, who would moderate the meetings, and who would speak to the press. We wanted a coherent and consistent position. We eventually came to consensus on each of these issues.

Then Curt and I drove to Truman's house. We sat in the basement with Truman, discussing his resignation statement. We talked through the events of the next morning. Where would Truman sit during church? Would he come in prior to the service or shortly after it started? Would he be there for Sunday school? In one respect, these seemed like insignificant points, but in light of what was about to happen, we all knew we had to pay attention to every detail.

Curt dropped me off at the Holiday Inn about 1:30 A.M. I still didn't know what I would preach. Normally I spend twenty hours in study for a Sunday sermon. I am not the kind who can stand up with minimal preparation and say something significant. That night, however, I read some Scriptures, prayed, and went to bed without knowing what I was going to say. I trusted that God would give me special wisdom for this important day.

The Announcement

As I sat on the platform, the past week seemed like an eternity. I had cried more in the last week than I had in years. And now the whirlwind was approaching the moment of resignation.

"I've preached in this pulpit many times," I began. "And I always look forward to being here, with the exception of today. I wouldn't have chosen to preach here today. But I'm going to anyway. And I have decided, for the sake of safety, to preach the sermon I preached last Sunday at Calvary Church. It's about David — and anyone else who ever made a mistake."

After my sermon, on David and Bathsheba, a staff member gave a public invitation for people to join the church. It seemed so odd to be concerned about church members when the pastor was about to resign. Nevertheless, several came forward with the desire to unite with the church.

At the end of the service, Curt stepped to the microphone and announced a special meeting of the church and graciously dismissed everyone who was not a member of the congregation. Since I had been asked by the deacons to be part of this unusual day, I stayed.

Truman, surrounded by his entire family, came to the microphone and read the statement of resignation.

When he finished, someone yelled from the audience, "Mr. Chairman, I move we refuse to accept this resignation."

A cheer erupted from the audience. Another man shouted support for Truman. It was immediately clear that the position of the deacons was dramatically different than the emotional response of the congregation. I knew in an instant that the situation could turn into a major conflict.

Before Curt could respond, Truman stepped to the microphone with a brief display of his strong leadership.

"That is not the issue," he said. "What I did was wrong, and whether you want me to pastor or not, I don't feel qualified to be your pastor. I am stepping down, and there is nothing you can do to change that. The deacons have done nothing that is improper."

Afterward, Truman stood in front of the altar, and people came by to hug him and say good-bye. For two and a half hours, I watched an incredible outpouring of love and feeling.

One of the staff members said, "This is awful!"

"No," I said. "This is important. This feeling has to be vented. Most people out there have messed up, many of them a whole lot worse than Truman. Anyone who has ever made a bad decision in life will throw arms around him and say, 'Thank God you're one of us.' "

Another person came up to me and said, "You whitewashed the whole situation. You even compromised the Scripture. You said in your sermon that David 'made a mistake.' King David didn't make a mistake; he *sinned*."

My emotions churned. How could anyone consider this whitewashing? The pastor admitted his action, confessed it publicly, asked the people to forgive him, and was now suffering the consequences of resignation. He was leaving the only thing he had done for thirty years. He was suffering public humiliation and embarrassment. He might never again return to pastoral ministry. And this guy thought we were whitewashing it? What more did he want? I felt hurt.

In the weeks that followed, I would learn that everyone had different reactions to the situation. In most such cases, I've learned, rarely is there unanimous support for *any* action.

I returned to the hotel exhausted. I opened my Bible to Galatians 6:1–8, the text I had decided would be the focus of my sermon for the evening.

Almost everyone came back to church that night. I preached ninety minutes. It was one of the most difficult sermons I have ever preached. I pledged publicly that I would stand with Truman through this crisis, to help "bear one another's burden." But I also preached that he was suffering the consequences of his behavior, that he had responsibility to "bear his own burden."

On the way home that evening, I was totally drained. I knew people had misunderstood my sermons during the day, but I was glad for the encouragement and support of the men from Calvary. I was so filled with insecurities, I talked the whole way home. I didn't want to be alone with my feelings and my thoughts; I wanted to sense from them that I had done and said the right things.

I lay down that night and wondered where Truman and Donna were. What were they thinking? What were they talking about? How were they feeling? It was a Father's Day I will never forget.

Donna's New Role

Life for Truman and Donna that week was incredibly hectic. People were in his house from early morning until the late hours of the evening. And the phone rang continuously. They received over five hundred long-distance phone calls.

Some life-long friends did not call, while people he had

known only casually — who had heard him speak at conferences or heard his tapes, read his books and articles — called several times. And there were the intimate friends who called often to comfort.

Knowing that his life was changing forever, Truman began to keep a daily diary. He wrote his feelings and observations. He recorded his reaction to Scriptures where he found comfort and instruction: "I believed it would be therapeutic for me. It was a very personal and private way to express myself. At times, it was as if I was writing about someone else, but I knew I was describing the collapse of my own life."

He wrote a series of observations in his diary, which he couched in what he called "Laws of Human Nature."

First law of human nature: The speed at which news spreads is directly related to its degree of badness.

Second law of human nature: When admitting something bad about oneself, the capacity to focus blame on others is infinite.

Third law of human nature: Nothing is totally appreciated until it is irretrievably lost.

Fourth law of human nature: Nothing you do in the future can erase the past; but with your life, you can give significance to the past.

He also bought an IBM-PC and began to write, but he says, "Most of the material I have never let anyone read."

I found out later some of the things that were happening to the Dollars. Among other things, an unlikely hero had emerged. Donna had always been a faithful and loving pastor's wife. She was also admired and loved by each congregation Truman served. She was, however, very quiet and lived in the background of Truman's more dominant pastoral and family role.

"As I led the church," Truman says, "she was always by my side, often in the shadows. In the home, I disciplined the children, handled the finances, and made almost all the decisions. This seemed to be in accord with her desire. It appeared to me she had chosen this quiet supporting role and that it best fitted her personality."

On the day Truman's life fell apart, though, she emerged as a strong figure by his side: "Her response was quick, decisive, and natural. She was supportive both in private and in public. She defended me, loved me, and comforted me. She became my great strength and constant partner.

"It was like she was transformed in a single day; and she has remained a strong help ever since. All four children were amazed at her sudden strength and admired her transformation."

Truman has since wondered how to explain this dramatic change. "I suppose it is like trying to explain how the pliable vice-president Harry Truman became the strong-willed president at Roosevelt's death. Some believe he was always strong and the new role gave him opportunity to display it. Others believe the pressure of the job made him strong.

"I am not sure what happened with Donna except I know it was a spiritual process, and without her sacrifice and support, restoration would not have been possible."

Short-Term Strategies

The initial crisis was over; however, the long process of putting the pieces back together was only beginning.

In a crisis situation, there are no timeouts. There is no quiet withdrawal from the whitewater to meditate and sort through what you are going to do. You must respond with haste and decision. The next week was a blur of events.

Looking back, I've identified several key tasks we had to handle immediately.

● *Help the congregation process the emotion.* When an event of this magnitude hits a congregation, people have to deal with questions, fears, and disillusionment. I encouraged the leaders at Temple to go overboard to give people opportunity to talk about this — to let it out, to express their feelings.

So for several weeks, they let people know that half a dozen deacons and staff would be at Temple Baptist each night between 7 and 9 P.M. to talk about the issues. But mostly they listened to, reassured, and prayed with people.

• *Control the flow of information to the media.* We didn't want a disjointed, inconsistent picture presented to the media, so we appointed one person to be the church spokesman. Whenever anyone needed information about Truman or the church's response, this person spoke officially on behalf of the church. Unfortunately, information was given to the media beyond the written statement. The failure to stick to the written statement resulted in front-page headlines that damaged the church and the people involved.

The papers hounded Truman for a response. Fortunately, he declined any comment because further comment from him would have given reporters more to talk about.

• *Control the curious.* Since the story was carried on the front page of the Detroit newspaper, it was not long before people called me from all over the country. The barrage of calls was more than I could possibly return.

"Preachers are probably the worst gossipers in the country," I said in disgust and despair one day. The worse the news, the more people wanted the inside details. All is done under the pretext of trying to help, of course, but in reality, I knew few of these people could offer any substantive help. Many people were angry at Truman, and I simply absorbed their wrath. I didn't pass any of those messages on to Truman.

Perhaps I was too cynical, but after a while, I returned only those calls from people I felt (1) genuinely cared about helping (not those who simply wanted the latest nuance of the story) and (2) had the resources necessary. In other words, I gave the details only to those who'd had a prior friendship with Truman, or people he respected, who I knew would call him to offer prayerful support.

With them, I'd tell the story and then say, "Why don't you call Truman directly? Here's the number where he can be reached."

The Long-Term Strategy

Restoration, to me, has two levels. The basic need is restoration to spiritual wholeness. Only after that issue is dealt with could we begin even to talk about the possibility of restoration to position.

We had no manual for managing such a crisis, nothing that

outlined appropriate steps for healing and restoration. But I was increasingly convinced of two facts: (1) Truman merited a legitimate process of restoration, to aid his own personal and spiritual healing and the healing of his important relationships, and (2) the process should occur within the authority and care of a local church.

I began discussing these ideas over the telephone with Truman. We decided to convene a small group of pastors to establish some guidelines and suggest a blueprint for this process.

The Pastors' Group

We agreed on four other pastors, and I called each of them: Jerry Falwell, Walt Handford, Jerry Thorpe, Harold Heninger. They gladly agreed to meet in Atlanta, Georgia, to consider the implications of Galatians 6:1 for this situation — "If someone is caught in a sin, you who are spiritual should restore him gently. But watch yourself, or you also may be tempted."

For the first hour and a half, Truman told his story. I noted a high level of skepticism by all the pastors. They didn't think he was telling the whole truth. Everybody assumed the worst — that he'd been physically involved. Several times Truman was interrupted by someone asking tough questions.

After lengthy discussion with Truman and then without him, the committee concluded there had been no physical involvement, only an indiscrete conversation by phone.

"Truman," said one of the group, "you've told us this is the honest truth. Now we need to be honest with you. Hear us well — if at any point in the future we receive information that proves your statements not to be totally truthful, we are out of the process. This whole thing is based on your being honest. And if at any point we find out you've been dishonest, we're out."

The committee independently confirmed Truman's story with all the people involved.

At the conclusion of the meeting, the pastors' group recommended the following steps:

1. Truman stop all public speaking and writing and resign

from all leadership positions.

2. Truman write a letter to the deacon board of Temple Baptist informing them that he would be submitting to the discipline of another church and that he would, under no circumstances, consider returning as pastor of Temple Baptist Church.

3. Truman and his wife should request a local church (preferably Calvary Church) to bring them under the discipline and care of that congregation. The following general guidelines were suggested:

— The board of that church should develop a specific strategy for their healing and restoration.

— This process should emphasize personal, spiritual growth for both Truman and Donna.

— The process of restoration should *not* have time limits.

— This process would not guarantee the type or place of future ministry.

— The possibility of future ministry would be recommended corporately by the church and the pastors to whom Truman had submitted.

— The leadership of Temple Baptist would provide input and advice during the restoration period.

4. A letter would be sent to Christian leaders around the country informing them of the steps that were taken in regard to Truman.

At first, Truman resisted the open-ended time frame. He suggested a six-month limit. He wanted an end in sight. But we insisted that the process would not guarantee any type or place of future ministry. We made clear that we were not going to guarantee Truman would ever be a pastor or leader again.

"We are committed," we said, "to restoring your relationship to God, your relationship to your family, your relationship to a community of believers, and your restoration to some type of meaningful service. But the question of leadership is not up to us. The possibility of future ministry will be recommended corporately by the church and by this committee."

This committee had no official ecclesiastical authority. Truman was not required to submit to our recommendations. The process of restoration rested totally with his voluntary compliance. He did so readily and completely. In my opinion, this was the single most significant factor in bringing about complete restoration.

Then I sent a letter to our church explaining the situation and the recommendations of the pastors' group. I also wrote:

On Sunday, July 24, Mr. and Mrs. Dollar met with the board of our church to discuss the possibility of coming under the care and discipline of our church. After a thorough meeting, the board unanimously and enthusiastically invited them to come under our care for a time of spiritual healing and restoration. A committee was formed to work with them during this process. The committee includes Mr. and Mrs. Jim DeVries (chairpersons), Mr. and Mrs. Dennis DeHaan, Mr. and Mrs. Ade VanWyk, Mr. and Mrs. Ken Ellis, and two couples from the board of Temple Baptist Church: Mr. and Mrs. Jay Hatfield and Mr. and Mrs. Curt Wilson.

We recognize that we have not walked this way before. We believe that we are following the spirit of Christ in this matter. We understand the process of restoration to involve three steps.

First, restoration to fellowship with God and others (2 Cor. 2:5–11, 1 John 1:9–10).

Second, restoration to service (the story of Peter's denial of Christ and his subsequent sermon at Pentecost).

Third, restoration to leadership. We are leaving this step up to God. We have made no commitment as to what Mr. Dollar can or cannot do after the restoration process.

I ask several things of our congregation. First, pray that God will lead us every step of the way. Second, pray for the Dollar family. We are committed to restoring them to spiritual health. We are leaving the issue of what they will do after that up to God. Third, pray that God will get the glory through this process. Fourth, please pray for me. As I have wept and prayed with the leaders of Temple Baptist Church and with each member of the Dollar family, I am reminded that I'm made of the same flesh. Pray that I will be true to God, my family, and the wonderful people of this congregation. I don't want to fail!

When you see Mr. and Mrs. Dollar in church, please make them feel at home. This will be a very difficult time for them. The words of Paul to the Corinthian church in regard to their response to a repentant brother have practical application for us: "The punishment inflicted on him by the majority is sufficient for him. Now instead, you ought to forgive and comfort him, so that he will not be overwhelmed by excessive sorrow. I urge you, therefore, to reaffirm your love for him."

The Restoration Committee

We felt that one of the real tests of Truman's repentance would be his willingness to submit to a group of lay people. This group, in the long run, was a crucial ingredient in the restoration process.

This group was appointed by the board of Calvary Church. Truman was not involved in picking the members. The fact that he was not in control of this process was important. He was not to tell us how to restore him; this group was going to tell him.

I knew the lay committee needed to be made up of people committed to restoration, but some of them needed to be skeptics. Just because they believed in restoration didn't mean they all thought Truman was going to get there. So we had a combination of assurers and doubters.

The group met with Truman and Donna Dollar once a month for about nine months, with no fixed agenda. Jim DeVries met with Truman about once a week.

The group was not a jury. Its primary purpose was to care, to love, to support the personal healing process, and to guide in vocational decisions.

Immediately, that meant helping Truman find work. The board at Temple Baptist had agreed to pay severance for a limited time. But Truman still needed something to do.

"The greatest pressure when you step out of ministry," Truman said to me one day, "is figuring out how to earn a living. You discover very quickly that the world out there is very unimpressed that you've been a pastor. You're essentially qualified to do nothing. The skills of ministry don't necessarily transfer into business."

I arranged with some business people in the church to get him an office. Even before he had a position, I felt he needed somewhere to go every day.

Eventually Truman linked up with business people, became a partner in some of their ventures, and ended up with a business of his own.

The lay committee also made sure the healing process continued.

After about three months, when life began to stabilize, the group recommended that Truman and Donna go to Marble Retreat, a facility in Colorado that offers pastors intensive therapy.

Again, the Dollars initially resisted, feeling that they were just beginning to regain emotional equilibrium — why stir up the pain all over again?

But the lay committee insisted: "You need to see if there are some root causes that brought this situation about. As a committee, we're not equipped to do that. We want you to probe the underlying drives, motivations, and fears that might cause this situation to recur in the future."

Those two weeks of focused help with psychiatrist Louis McBurney became a key turning point in the recovery process. Not only did their cooperation show that Truman and Donna were committed to the restoration process, but they both came back able to point to specific things they gained from the experience.

Truman, for instance, had to sense deeply that his significance and value to God is not determined by whether he's in ministry or by the size of his church. He had to accept both emotionally and intellectually that there's more to life than work.

He also learned more clearly the importance of a personal relationship with God, not just a professional relationship with God.

"For the last three years," Truman told me recently, "I have read the Bible and prayed because *I* needed to read the Bible and pray. For thirty years before that, I read the Bible and prayed, allegedly because I needed to, but I was really doing it for everybody else."

In short, he learned balance. He's now convinced that it's okay to take time off to relax, to exercise, to spend time with his family — to be something *besides* a pastor of a big church.

Yet another role of the committee was to resist the temptation to short-circuit the process and announce complete restoration too soon. One of the tests of Truman's repentance was his willingness to bring to this group things he needed their counsel on, and to submit to their wisdom. He clearly demonstrated that.

The Pastoral Connection

Some people feel that if a pastor messes up, restoration means taking him to rock bottom, stripping him of dignity and worth, forcing him to rebuild.

I felt otherwise. In Truman's case, the process of resigning and being on the front page of the Detroit newspaper was humiliation enough. I didn't want deliberately to add to the humiliation he'd already brought on himself. To do so would likely bring about bitterness and loss of hope.

So, while not part of the committee, I called Truman several times a week to keep in touch. I must confess that, amid this flurry of activity, it was difficult to concentrate on the responsibilities I had as pastor of Calvary Church. In the early stages of the process, I welcomed the challenge of this additional pressure. But the longer the process went, the more effort it required. Yet I felt compelled to do it.

I was committed to preserving Truman's dignity. I was calling him to let him know that our relationship was the same. He wasn't a pastor anymore, but he was still my friend. If I was struggling with decisions in the church, I'd run my concerns by him. I didn't care if he'd messed up. He still had wisdom.

But we usually ended up talking about what he was going through, which was an overwhelming sense of loss and worthlessness. These visits took a lot of my time; nevertheless I felt they were important.

In the days since, Truman has indicated that these informal

conversations, and his conversations with Jim DeVries, during which they would read Scripture and pray, were some of the most important in the restoration process.

Truman now says that Jim DeVries is "the first real friend I've ever had." Everybody else has been "a friend with conditions, a friend because of ministry." But Jim, according to Truman, is the first guy he's met in his entire life who accepts and loves him as a person, not as a preacher or church leader.

Jim's continuing contact was key in gauging Truman's progress.

When Is Restoration Complete?

Ultimately, in the restoration process, you've got to make a judgment call. Because discernment is so difficult, a group needs to be involved — no individual is capable of seeing the whole picture.

After eighteen months, we reviewed the steps we had seen:

1. Truman's willingness to accept the authority of the lay committee and to be accountable, demonstrated when the committee rejected his desire to re-enter ministry prematurely.

2. Truman's willingness to accept professional counseling and embrace an examination of his spiritual and emotional foundation.

3. Truman's willingness to accept fully secular employment as a long-term option. The longer the process went, the less insistent he became of returning to pulpit ministry.

4. Truman's evidence of contrition. Truman had always been one to dominate a group by the force of his personality. Now, he didn't have to be center stage; he no longer tried to run the meetings. Instead of directing the conversation, he was hesitant to speak, and when he did, it was often with deep emotion.

He confessed, "There are times when I am sitting in my office in the middle of conducting business, and I close the door and just break down and weep uncontrollably. This is now almost three years later. I am still overwhelmed with the awfulness, not just of what I did, but what my actions brought about in my family and the church and the cause of Christ."

After reviewing these developments, the lay committee recommended to Calvary Church that the Dollars be accepted as members without any restrictions on service, which meant that they could teach, lead, serve, and perform any of the normal functions within the local church.

This cleared the way for the pastors' committee to clear Truman to accept a leadership position. Shortly thereafter, the ministerial group met and removed its previous recommendations of restraint. We knelt together and laid hands on Truman and prayed over him. We encouraged him to get involved in ministry again.

The pastoral committee unanimously agrees that Truman is now free to accept a leadership position, but our understanding is that any decision will be made with the advice and consent of the committee.

I don't think the process of restoration is ever finished. Our formal involvement, which has seen him back to health, to stability, to restoration, has ended. But in my opinion, Truman will wrestle with these issues for the rest of his life. But now more than ever he knows personally the grace and healing power of God.

> *Pastors have a measure of control over how the storm of*
> *controversy affects them and their church.*
> — *Edward Dobson*

CHAPTER TEN

When the Church Is in the Headlines

In the early 1970s, I pastored a small church in a West Virginia mountain town of 7,000 people. During this time controversy raged over school textbooks. Many Christians felt that the books were subtly projecting values that, in some cases, were contrary to Christian values. To some extent, I agreed with them, so I decided to get involved.

I bought an advertisement in the newspaper to announce that my next Sunday night sermon would address the issue. A big crowd, with many visitors, flocked to the service, and I said some inflammatory things. From that day on I stood facing a raging storm.

I had decided not to fight with the school board over the content of the books; instead I set my sights on a more permanent solution: I wanted to push for the inclusion of parents in the process of textbook selection. So after my Sunday night sermon, I organized a pastors' meeting, including both Catholics and Protestants, and I invited the media. Their coverage of that event gave me my first taste of being quoted out of context. Because of my youthful enthusiasm and comments about public education, I came across to some as a sweat-drenched, anti-intellectual fanatic.

The controversy came to a head at a school board meeting attended by seemingly the entire town. It was a long, wild night, with people losing their tempers and shouting accusations. When the vote was finally taken, the board agreed to include the parents in decision making.

For those who would settle for nothing short of the incineration of all the questionable materials, this was a defeat. They vowed to continue the fight. Since I had accomplished my goal, however, I pulled out of the controversy, only to earn myself the label of "compromiser" with some people.

A public controversy is a tropical hurricane. Powerful, destructive winds blow beyond the control of any individual or church. Total disaster is a real possibility.

In a hurricane, wise residents on the coastlands take full protective measures, packing up their belongings and driving inland, taping their windows and covering them with plywood, stocking up food in the basement.

Church controversies can take many forms. Even internal controversies can sometimes become public. But whatever the cause of the controversy, pastors and churches can take protective measures when they face public storms in ministry.

Avoiding Needless Public Controversy

I have no shortage of experience with ministry hurricanes. I left the West Virginia church to work as spokesman for Jerry Falwell during the organizing of the Moral Majority. I participated in count-less forums and talk shows and weathered many public crises with him. That experience has shaped my perception of public controversies.

In particular, I now avoid public controversy at all costs. I see the church's community role primarily as evangelism, so anything that hinders the spreading of the gospel is out.

Naturally, a lot of controversy is out of our hands. Sometimes a church gets sued or threatens to split or has something immoral happen within its walls. When such information is made public, the church has to deal with it publicly.

But we can avoid needless controversy.

When I've involved myself in political issues, for example, people have categorized me; they've labeled me; they've associated me with one party or another. And that shut me off from large segments of the community, especially those who disagreed with my political views.

So I take deliberate steps to avoid being pigeon-holed. I tell people that on some issues I'm a liberal, on others a conservative; on some I'm an evangelical, on others a fundamentalist; on some I'm a Republican, on others a Democrat. I want our church to be known for spiritual issues, for helping people in the community, not for things easily politicized.

I recognize that other pastors want to be the conscience of the community. Being the salt of the earth, for them, means confronting the world with the truth on spiritual *and* social issues. The church is not only a force for evangelism in the world but also a cultural preservative, even among those who will never be converted. In this view, controversy is inevitable, even desirable. But when your goal is evangelism, this just won't do.

Still, there are times I feel compelled to speak out on sensitive social issues. But before I speak out, I make sure that we are involved in helping those affected by the problem.

Several years ago Harold Ivan Smith came to town to speak at our church, and in the course of our conversation I learned that his father had caught AIDS from a blood transfusion and died. So I asked

Harold to speak about AIDS in the Sunday morning service. His message heightened our awareness of the problem, and we sensed a need for a written AIDS policy for our church.

After considerable study, we established the policy, "We will not discriminate against people with AIDS but extend to them the love and grace of Christ."

Afterward I drove to the AIDS resource center in Grand Rapids, a purely secular agency, and said, "We want to get involved with helping people with AIDS."

They said, "Frankly, people like you are the last people we would figure to come here and offer help." We were only the third church in the community to do so. They introduced me to several people, one of whom I brought with me to our monthly board meeting. He had the disease. I asked him to tell his story, and by the time he finished everyone in the room was in tears. He now attends our church, as do others with AIDS.

I can now make a public statement about AIDS that would have weight even with the people in the homosexual community. They know we do not accept homosexuality as a biblical expression of human sexuality, but they see we're down there with homosexuals who have AIDS. We aren't simply judging others.

Only in this way have I been able to speak on controversial issues without raising the level of controversy. In addition, I've found that I can pursue successfully some controversial issues without making a public issue out of my involvement.

Some good has come out of the West Virginia textbook controversy — a subcommittee of teachers, parents, and board members still reviews all the textbooks. But I now see that we could have achieved the same objectives without being on the front page and without alienating people.

Dealing with the Congregation

Even though I try to avoid unnecessary controversy, I still find myself in the midst of it from time to time. In dealing with it, so that the hurricane doesn't destroy the church, I've found it best to concentrate my attention on each of the parties involved.

The Truman Dollar crisis at Temple Baptist (see chapter nine) illustrates how a public crisis aggravates internal pressures in a church. A church can weather a public controversy if it can prevent a mutiny. Here are six things we found helpful in that situation.

• *Present a united front to the public.* If leaders and members in the church are saying different things to the media, it fractures the church into parties and opinions. I told the Temple Baptist board that (1) they should designate one spokesperson to the press so the press would know whom to call, and (2) they should prepare a single written statement for the church and the media. By working together to write and edit the statement, leaders understand one another better, and they own the church's position.

• *Coach the congregation.* The people in church need to have some understanding of the press. Controversy makes great headlines; peace and unity is not news. The press has a responsibility to present objectively all sides of an issue.

At Temple Baptist, as you would expect, the press interviewed people coming out of services, playing one person's views off against another:

"Pastor Dobson thinks this; do you agree?"

"As far as we can tell, three of the church deacons believe so-and-so. Do you know of any others in the church who oppose that idea?" That can inflame more disagreement and divide a congregation.

Most people in the church don't realize what's happening with the press. They're enamored that a reporter is talking to them, that their names may get in the paper. At the same time, they're intimidated by reporters and say things they shouldn't. Therefore I coach the congregation about what we prefer they say and not say, do and not do, and why.

I can't be dictatorial, however. I emphasize that people are free to say what they want, but usually we prefer they respond to reporters with "You need to talk to our church spokesperson. Do you have his name and number?"

• *Stop those rumors.* There will never be an information

vacuum. Curious people will talk, and someone will supply information, true or false, rumor or conjecture or gossip; so it is best for leaders to supply truth. In addition, any misinformation arising from gossip or the media needs to be rebutted.

At Temple Baptist, the church deacons were available at the building every night so members could get direct information. A business meeting closed to outsiders and the press is also beneficial.

● *Encourage people to pray.* This has two benefits. First, we need God to solve the problem. Second, people turn their attention and energies in a positive and constructive direction. Prayer points their eyes where they need to be, on God rather than on people and problems.

● *Handle the problem in special business meetings rather than in preaching.* Since the controversy is on a pastor's mind, it is natural to preach about it, but I think that's a mistake.

I've noticed that the more controversy preachers address from the pulpit, the more people screen their messages, asking, "Who is he saying this to?" People then read between the lines, filtering everything through the current controversy. Rather than assuming the pastor is speaking to them for their strengthening and edification, they assume he or she has an agenda. So people distance themselves from the preached word.

So I do everything possible to separate the controversy from worship services. I hold business meetings in a different room if possible, and not as an addendum to the morning service.

In the worship service I'll say, "We're going through a tough time. You may have read the paper; I have no comments about that this morning. However, we will hold a special meeting for members this afternoon, and the board will make a statement and answer questions. This morning's sermon has absolutely no relationship to that."

Dealing with the Press

Since most churches rarely deal with the press, they can be caught off guard when the media starts paying attention to them. How they handle the press, of course, can make a huge difference in how they handle their controversy.

One of the keys to dealing effectively with the press is anticipation and preparation. I make several decisions ahead of time.

• *Be honest.* Honesty is right in itself, of course, but it also bears directly on your relationship to the press. Their job is truth. Their job is to investigate, to uncover, to get the story. If they suspect a cover up, there's blood in the water, and they become sharks. On the other hand, once they sense they have the story, they're gone. There is no more news to be had.

For example, politicians who have done something wrong usually ride out the storm of adverse public opinion if they are honest. The press headlines the story today, and tomorrow they headline something else. Soon the misdeed is forgotten. But politicians who have been dishonest with the press watch their problems being regurgitated over and over on the front page.

• *Be forthright.* Forthrightness doesn't mean you tell everything you know about a situation; it means that you don't imply you've given all the information when you haven't.

At times I'll have to inform the press, "I cannot tell you all the details about this story," and then I'll tell them why I can't.

At Liberty University, for example, sometimes a student was expelled for immoral behavior. That was news in Lynchburg, so the press would sometimes ask for details. But I wouldn't tell them why an athlete was cut from the football team or why a student was expelled from the university — students have the right to privacy, I'd say. We would tell the press, "You will have to talk to the student."

Another reason not to give all the information is potential litigation. Whatever the reason for withholding information, though, it must be legitimate.

• *Choose a spokesperson of good judgment.* As I mentioned, the church needs to hammer out exactly what it wants to say about the controversy it finds itself in, and then it needs to appoint a spokesperson to address the press about its decision. That spokesperson must give only the information the church has decided to give.

Suffice it to say that the spokesperson needs to be carefully chosen. He or she must have good judgment and discretion, knowing intuitively what is appropriate and inappropriate.

The person should be capable of answering a reporter's question in one or two sentences. A spokesperson who needs paragraphs to answer a question will (a) likely say more than has been agreed on, and (b) give the reporter more room to edit, which often leads to being quoted out of context.

Although the pastor is the natural choice, he or she may not be the right choice because of pastors' tendency to "talk long." I prefer a laconic member of the board.

A church also needs to decide whether the spokesperson who reads the statement will (1) read the statement without comment, or (2) read the statement and answer questions about its contents. At a minimum, the spokesperson should not answer questions about topics outside the scope of the written statement.

● *Keep key assumptions in mind.* Whoever happens to be speaking to the press, it's vital that the person keep in mind five assumptions:

1. The press doesn't understand the church. An editor assigns to a story a reporter who doesn't have time for heavy research in theology, polity, and church history. Reporters are a blank slate at best and a bit biased at worst.

So we must communicate at the level they will understand. I can't use church jargon. I never assume they understand the difference between evangelicals and fundamentalists or why I am generally opposed to divorce and remarriage.

2. I lose control of my words after the press gets them. Once I give an interview, once I answer questions over the phone, once I talk at a press conference, reporters can edit my words at will and print what they have chosen without my approval.

I have learned, then, that the less I say, the less room reporters have to edit. So I use a written statement, and that dramatically decreases the chances of being misquoted, of saying more than I intend, and of being misunderstood.

3. The press never writes what you expect. The press has a different perspective and different goals. What is important to you is often irrelevant and boring to the media; what is threatening to you is news to them. You want to maintain your reputation; they are not in the reputation business. You want the community to see your church as a place of health, strength, and love; the press searches for conflict and problems.

I don't think the press deliberately distorts what happens in a church. There isn't a conspiracy to make Christians look stupid. More often than not we make ourselves look stupid. Knowing human nature, I recognize there will be some bias, but that bias won't kill us. If I keep this in mind, I won't be devastated when the news about my church is reported differently than I would wish.

4. *The press will eventually hear everything I tell church members.* Information is like spilled milk. Even if we hold a closed-door meeting for members, church people talk, and I can't muzzle them. I never assume they will keep mum if a reporter calls. In fact, there seems to be an inverse relationship between the sensitivity of information and your ability to cap the bottle once you tell others.

5. *News too will pass.* When an unfavorable story runs in the paper, it feels like the end of the world. "Thousands of people are reading this," we moan. "The church is ruined. No visitor will ever come again!"

But the reality is that a church with integrity will eventually carry the day, because especially in large communities, within a month, people won't remember which church the story was about. And they'll probably not even remember the "scandal," for fresh news is being trumpeted before them every day.

● *Don't attack the press.* The worst case scenario is not an unfavorable story in the press; the worst case scenario is war with the press. So even when the story is scrambled and I'm misquoted, I never pull up broadside and exchange cannon fire. You can't win.

"Never fight with someone who buys ink by the barrel," said Sam Rutigliano, former coach of the Cleveland Browns and now head coach at Liberty University.

If the press has egregiously erred, I call the paper, state my case, and request a retraction. But I know the retraction will be buried near the obituaries, and the average reader doesn't care.

(When was the last time you read a retraction?) Their only value is as evidence if you are confronted by an individual who uses the original but false information to criticize the church.

And in the rare case when the media does try to manipulate me, I've still found it best to challenge them privately.

Several years ago I debated the head of Fundamentalists Anonymous on a TV program aired in Cleveland. The moderator took questions from a small audience in the studio. One woman stood up and said, "I'm a Jew; are you telling me that if I don't accept Jesus Christ I'm going to hell?"

People had asked that question everywhere I went, and I answered it as I had dozens of times before. I discovered after the show, however, that she was an employee of the station, planted in the audience and told what to ask. The question didn't bother me, but the manipulation did.

Several months later I did the program again. Before it started, I told the interviewer, "I don't mind answering any questions people have, but I don't appreciate that when I was here last, you had one of your employees sit out there acting as if she was part of the audience."

He smiled, but he got the point.

Still, in our information age, it's usually not worth confronting a faulty press. And usually it doesn't matter: to most people, news goes in one ear and out the other.

● *Let your good works shine.* Sometimes churches are tempted to counteract bad press by running an advertising campaign, to improve their image. I've never found that to be effective. 1 Peter 2:15 says, "By doing good you should silence the ignorant talk of foolish men." Attempts to improve public image through an advertising blitz will be seen for what they are, and they'll waste money. It is our integrity and commitment to helping people in need that wins the respect of outsiders. In the long run, for a community-serving church a public controversy is just a blip on the screen.

● *Bring in the gospel whenever possible.* Even if the situation becomes a circus, I find some way to insert the Good News. I concern myself more with the gospel finding an open door than with maintaining my image or the church's image.

A number of years ago I was on the Phil Donahue show. When I was introduced the audience booed. I was defending the Boy Scouts who had dismissed an eagle scout who was an atheist. It was a knockdown-dragout hour. However, I did have the opportunity of briefly sharing what it means to believe in God and have a relationship with him.

Dealing With the Law

Most pastors don't intentionally or knowingly break the law, so we may be prone to give it less consideration than we should. Any public relations crisis has the potential to be a legal crisis. Through some hard experiences, I've learned two lessons about legal matters.

● *Whenever in doubt, check with your lawyer.* A married university student who attended our church put her child in our nursery. Before long the nursery workers suspected child abuse and informed me. When I confronted the father, he admitted it. We secured a licensed psychologist to care for him and put the child under a physician's treatment. We intended to report it to the local government agency, but because we had placed the parents and child under professional care, we delayed the notification.

Big mistake. The father abused the child again. This time the government agencies found out, and I was arrested for failure to report suspected child abuse.

I went to court, and the judge cleared me of all liability, but I learned a painful lesson: don't mess with the law. Although a pastor may have a casual attitude toward the fine points of the law and not get burned for decades, one law suit can cost tens of thousands of dollars and waste uncounted hours, not to mention the public embarrassment.

So when in doubt, especially with church discipline cases, I phone our lawyer. That call costs money, but it could save much, much more later on.

● *Guard against libel.* One legal pitfall of any public controversy is libel. A safeguard against inadvertent libel is a phrase I learned while working as spokesman for Moral Majority; Jerry Falwell's lawyers hammered at me to preface everything with, "In my opinion." Apparently, according to the law, everyone is entitled to an opinion, and that little phrase alleviates you and the organization from liability.

The relentless, overwhelming power of a hurricane is a frightening thing. Unlike a tornado, a hurricane seems like it will last forever. But eventually the swirling, low pressure zone moves inland; no longer fueled by the heat of the ocean, the winds peter out.

And gradually, out from their basements and shelters come the residents of the windswept area. They find destruction, all right. But if they've taken the right steps, the damage to their homes and property has been limited. After a few weeks of clean-up and repair, their lives go on as if the hurricane had never hit.

So it is with a public controversy well-handled.

*Just as a doctor can resort to ice packs for a sprained ankle
and antibiotics for an infection, so I can bring factors to
bear in a dispute that will encourage the disputing parties
to seek their own healing.*

— Edward Dobson

CHAPTER ELEVEN

Reconciling Battling Members

One young man in our church, a fairly new believer employed
by another member in our church, resigned his job with the understanding that the company owed him a sizeable sum of money.

Months passed, and the owner, a long-standing member of
our church, refused to pay. Finally, rather than sue, John lodged a
complaint with the Restoration and Healing Committee of our
church. After six months of mediation, both parties agreed to a
settlement of 20 percent of the original sum.

Months passed, and we were told that the owner of the company would not pay up. So the church board got involved again. The committee voted to discipline the company owner, barring him from ministry in church and placing his membership on hold.

Saturday night at 10 P.M. he called me at home and demanded to see me immediately.

Like it or not, pastors at times are firefighters. And it doesn't take a ten-alarm fire to scorch a pastor — a flickering match can inflict third-degree burns, and a smoldering mattress can kill through smoke inhalation.

Whether members feud over something as minor as Mary forgetting to invite Betty to her tea or something as major as thousands of dollars, the pastor risks hurting feelings, feeding opposition agendas, making enemies, creating factions.

So why hazard it? Why not just let people handle their own problems?

Why Risk Getting Burned?

Actually, most of the time I don't get involved. In our church we have established a Committee for Restoration and Healing, which at any one time is handling twelve to fifteen cases: threatened divorce, business disputes, interpersonal strife. I'm not on that committee. They resolve most situations without my input.

But not all. Though I had scrupulously avoided being sucked into the dispute described above, when the owner of the business phoned me on that Saturday night, I had to act.

When we met, he maintained, "I really don't owe him the money."

After some discussion, I replied, "You agreed to this settlement. You signed off on it, and you haven't met your commitment."

The following week he cut a check. Both men and their wives, formerly close friends, met with me. They apologized to each other, asked forgiveness, hugged, and prayed.

A pastor can sometimes be the deciding factor in such a resolution. He may not say or do anything different than others; simply by the weight of position and spiritual authority, he breaks the deadlock.

That can mean better spiritual health for the individuals involved and greater unity for the church. Such reconciliation doesn't happen automatically. I've learned a few things over the years, though, that make it more of a possibility.

Mistakes to Avoid

I have found that three mistakes will turn peacemaking perilous.

● *To mediate alone.* One woman in our church, a member, filed for divorce against her husband, which automatically involved her with the Committee for Restoration and Healing. They met with her and her husband, and they concluded that the couple had no biblical basis for divorce.

They informed her of their decision, offered support and counseling services, and in accordance with church policy, said, "For the next twelve months, you will be an inactive member of the church. During that time you need to work toward a biblical resolution of this conflict. After twelve months, if you have not resolved it, the church will be forced to drop you from membership."

She aborted the process, withdrawing her membership. However, a year later she remarried and returned to the church. At that time we did something that in retrospect I think was unwise. The elders wrote her a letter: "You are not welcome here until you face up to the unresolved situation when you withdrew your membership." We didn't want her to divorce her new husband but simply to acknowledge, "Yes, I have strayed from God's will, and I'm sorry."

A week later we decided that ours had been a stupid move, that we were not prepared to try to stop people from attending. So the chairman of the board and I met with the couple. She defended her actions as biblical. We disagreed with her and said they could attend the church if she and her new husband wished, but we also told her we would not accept them into membership without an acknowledgement of wrongdoing.

She replied, "We still plan to come."

They attended for a while. Eventually they stopped, and the last I heard, she had retained an attorney and was considering suing us for discrimination against divorced people.

When predicaments like this arise, I'm always relieved I haven't tackled the dispute alone. Nothing can be more dangerous for a pastor. Group intervention is advisable for three reasons:

1. There's wisdom in a multitude of counselors. In this case, we determined our every step based on the wisdom of the group. One man would bring up a point, another a counterpoint, then a consensus would emerge. The group's collective wisdom surpassed anything I would have decided on my own.

2. There's protection in numbers. When situations get ugly, a pastor needs the legal protection of the board and the corporate status of the church.

3. Numbers dilute the possibility of the dispute narrowing into a personal conflict — me versus another person. The decisions are decisions of the church, not my decisions. Sometimes the final agreement will be unfavorable to one or both parties, so one or both will be dissatisfied or bitter. The pastor who tackles it alone is in a no-win situation.

• *To take sides.* One pastor I know made this mistake in marriage counseling. The husband and wife both were drinkers, but the woman was an alcoholic. In one session, after the husband had complained about how her drinking was weakening his commitment to the marriage and how their teenage kids detested their mother, the pastor took the side of the husband.

"If you don't get a hold of yourself," he said to her, "you may lose your family. You've got to take responsibility for your actions."

That may have been true, but the moment the words left his mouth, he realized he had blundered. The husband, who was no saint, felt justified, and the wife felt attacked from all sides. She never returned to counseling with that pastor.

Each side in a controversy desperately wants the pastor to be the judge (and to rule in their favor, of course). To such couples, I have learned to say, with Jesus, "Who appointed me a judge or an arbiter between you?" I assure them, "I am here to help *you* resolve this issue."

I or the committee can't resolve other people's conflicts. We can't agree for them. We can't forgive for them. If there is going to be true reconciliation and peace, the combatants must achieve it.

● *To rush into intervention.* Although doing nothing can allow small fires to enlarge, a pastor rushing to resolve a conflict can cause equal or greater problems.

1. For small problems or petty conflicts, a pastor's intrusion can be too threatening and heavy handed. Knowing that the pastor will call every time they have a tiff with another may scare some people out of the church. Nobody wants a busy-body for a pastor.

2. The pastor's involvement in a dispute can inflate a conflict between individuals into a church-wide problem. As leader of the church, anything I do or say has the potential of becoming a church issue, and thus a potentially divisive or polarizing issue. Others can perceive me as throwing my weight around or abusing power, giving ammunition to those who are already opponents of my leadership.

One pastor I know tried prematurely to resolve a conflict between four leaders in the women's group. The problem had smoldered as a personality conflict but ignited when they disagreed over program plans for their monthly meetings. When the pastor tried to settle the feud by publicly backing the decision of the leader, he suddenly found himself the enemy of the other three women. Soon their husbands also opposed him, and within months nearly every committed leader in his small church had left.

3. In a small church especially, if a pastor involves himself frequently in conflict resolution, he will find himself mediating more and more disputes. Even squabbling children instinctively know how to get clout on their side, running to their parents with tears in their eyes. The more pastors settle fights, the more they fan the flames of sibling rivalry, and the more they will be called on to referee.

4. Maturity involves learning to settle disputes we have with others. I'm not helping my people to grow in Christ if I jump in and try to help them solve each of their problems. They've got to learn to work these things out for themselves. I want to be there when things threaten to get out of hand; that, after all, is one of the

purposes of the church — to be there in crises. But it's also a purpose of the church to help people to mature in faith. And that means, most of the time, letting people settle their conflicts themselves.

The Stages of Intervention

Most disputes are complex, with combatants stubbornly crouching in their bunkers, so I have to coax people to the peace table in stages.

● *Determine whether intervention is necessary.* Naturally, this is a judgment call. But in general, if the dispute has been ongoing and is beginning to affect the church body, then it's time to try to intervene.

An argument between the Sunday school superintendent and a Sunday school teacher about the lack of crayons in the supply room is one thing. When the Sunday school teacher and the superintendent start telling other teachers about the stubbornness of the other, creating suspicion and anger in a whole department, then it's probably time to step in.

This applies whether or not the parties involved come to me or our committee. Just because someone approaches us with a conflict doesn't mean it's worth the committee's time. And just because people don't come to the committee doesn't mean we won't step in. It depends on how destructive the conflict could become.

This rule also applies to cases that don't directly involve other members. For instance, divorce proceedings may appear to be a private affair. But if the man or wife is involved in leadership, then the church's integrity is at stake. If the couple can't resolve their differences, then whether or not they approach the church, we will attempt to intervene.

● *See whether the parties are willing to end the fight.* Just because we think intervention is necessary doesn't mean we will proceed with it. Our experience has shown that unless the parties involved are willing to end their fighting, there's no point in going through a resolution process. The antagonists need to admit that their dispute displeases God and that they need to do something about it. If they can't see that, there's no point in seeking resolution. Church discipline becomes the only option.

● *Negotiate a process agreeable to both parties.* Although we offer some guidelines for a resolution process, the parties have to negotiate the process themselves. If we simply impose a process on them, they are much less likely to agree with the outcome.

The parties have to agree on what they are going to decide, what steps they'll take in deciding it, and who will help them decide. If either party is uncomfortable with one or more members of the restoration committee, we'll let them bring in a person they do trust.

In other words, we're pretty flexible at this point, as long as the parties aren't stalling and are putting together a process they can both agree to.

In the case of the two men involved in the business dispute explained in the introduction, they agreed at this point that they would submit to the process of negotiation as well as abide by the recommendations that were made.

● *Require a commitment to submit to the process whatever the results.* If the parties have agreed on the process, we assume they will submit to the results. But in any case, we want them to say so — it's another step of commitment to resolving the dispute. Saying this up front also reminds people that they better have been serious in negotiating the process — they are literally going to have to live with it.

In addition, we caution them, "You probably will not agree with everything decided, but since mature, biblical, and objective people will be mediating, the settlement will be as fair as possible. The only way to achieve reconciliation is through give and take on both sides. You can reconcile without agreeing on all the details."

It was only because we took this step that we were able to get the employer to pay his former employee. He was reneging until I forcefully reminded him of his promise earlier in the negotiations.

● *Execute the mediation process.* Sometimes this can take six months to a year. Along the way, each party may put roadblocks in the way. The process may require meeting with the aggrieved parties separately as well as together.

For example, recently an employer who is a member of our church dismissed one of his secretaries who is also a member of our church. She filed an age–discrimination suit against him with the local employment commission. She also notified the church of her actions.

We met with her and requested she remove her claim from the public forum and let the church mediate her situation. She agreed to do that, and her employer agreed to our mediation. It took several individual meetings before the parties were brought together and the problem solved. The mediation also included an expert on employee relations and the law.

• *Bring closure to the reconciliation.* Beyond dousing the flames, we seek to restore the relationship. After the settlement, we encourage the former foes to join in Communion with the mediation committee. This may involve seeking forgiveness from each other. In some cases, it takes several hours to confess and resolve many hurts. When one conflict between two businessmen was resolved, they met together, asked forgiveness, cried, and hugged.

The Pastor's Role in Intervention

An acquaintance of mine told me something a doctor told him: "Doctors don't heal the body; the body heals itself. Sometimes a disease or infection becomes more than the body can handle on its own. With the medication and procedures we use, we are trying to give the body a chance to heal itself."

In conflict mediation, I see my role in similar terms. I can't coerce people to reconcile. But just as a doctor can resort to ice packs for a sprained ankle and antibiotics for an infection, so I can bring factors to bear in a dispute that will encourage the disputing parties to seek their own healing. These are:

• *Scripture.* Sometimes a pastor feels he exerts no more authority than the referee of a World Wrestling Federation match. However, while the WWF doesn't exactly stand behind its referees, God wholly backs up his Word.

Scripture is the strongest factor influencing people to begin and continue the painful process of reconciliation. God-fearing people, convinced that conflict and bitterness displease God, will swallow their pride and make peace with enemies. It doesn't take more than a few gentle reminders, especially from Ephesians, to encourage people to reconcile.

My use of Scripture, of course, depends on the clarity of the Scripture. When the verse under question is clear (for example, that stealing is wrong), I state my position unequivocally.

When a verse is subject to two or more interpretations (for example on the divorce issue), I explain my interpretation and clearly label it as such. I don't try to strong-arm them into buying my interpretation but insist that they decide what they think is right. I leave the issue between them and God, because that's where the issue ultimately rests (it's *their* conflict). I never get embroiled in an argument over correct interpretation.

● *Motivation.* By approaching the parties in conflict and saying, "Let's try to work this out," I serve as an instigator and impetus of reconciliation. Just as a preacher brings people, especially people who otherwise avoid that decision, to the point of faith with an "altar call," so I beckon adversaries with a "peacemaking call."

● *Productive communication.* Until they start talking, rivals cannot reconcile. But when opponents try to communicate on their own, they often lock horns and do more goring than good. They accuse, threaten, and yell.

In the presence of a pastor, they are much less likely to behave in the same way. A church committee can perform this same service, but there's also something about the office of pastor that puts people on their best behavior. In some pastoral situations, that reality makes me squirm — I usually don't like people to put on a false front when I'm around. But when I stand between two angry people, I'm thankful for the forbearance that my office encourages.

● *Accountability.* On occasion, I've had to warn warring members that they were jeopardizing their opportunities and privileges in church by their ongoing strife. If they don't settle, I tell them, they'll forfeit leadership roles, ministry functions (such as choir), and ultimately church membership.

I'm not waving a stick at that time; I'm simply informing them of the implications of their stubbornness. No one should minister whose spiritual life is crippled by a refusal to restore relationships. No one should continue as a member who blatantly ignores Scripture and church leaders. And although committee members can bring others to accountability in this way, sometimes it takes a word from the pastor to drive the point home.

The Special Case of Staff Conflict

Conflict between staff has many of the same dynamics as does conflict between members. I see only a couple of things that need to be kept in mind. In particular, most staff conflict is due to one of two causes:

1. Lack of communication. Staff members assume what other staff members may or may not be doing.

2. Getting cornered. Staff members take a position and then can't gracefully back down.

One Sunday night the bathrooms were backed up by paper towels in the commode. The custodians blamed the young people, though they didn't have witnesses. They came to the youth pastor and said, "You've got to control those kids."

"Did you see any young people even go in there?" he asked.

"No, we didn't see them."

Well, that led our business administrator to rekey every door in the building. He restricted pastors' access to certain areas of the building, and to prevent kids entering after their activities, he denied the youth pastor a key to the front door of the building. The result was mistrust and palpable animosity.

Finally, I convened our management team of seven people and our ministry leaders and said, "This key stuff is a pain in the neck. Let's talk it out."

In that setting everyone involved was more flexible, and we resolved the problem quickly.

I have found that most staff conflict can be solved by getting people to sit down and talk by themselves. If they have tried and cannot settle the dispute on their own, I offer to sit down with them and mediate the problem.

In contrast to mediating with others in the church, I am much more willing to mediate alone between staff members. For one thing, I see that as part of my responsibility as head of staff. For another, there are unique staff dynamics that should remain confidential.

I didn't enter the ministry to settle scuffles. I get frustrated when I have to take time away from preaching, evangelism, and discipleship in order to hose down fires. But ministry boils down to relationships, to individuals working together in harmony. Positive, peaceful relationships are the building blocks of a strong church. As a result, conflict resolution is more than bleak necessity: "Blessed are the peacemakers, for they will be called sons of God."

Part 5
Conflict Redeemed

Pastoral ministry demands a high emotional investment,
especially in times of tension, and sometimes you wonder
if there's a return.

— *Marshall Shelley*

CHAPTER TWELVE

The Exacting Price
of Ministry

W illiam Barclay defined a saint as "*someone whose life makes it easier to believe in God.*" For a pastor caught in the middle of conflict, it's easy to question whether you're doing any good for God at all. You find yourself questioning not only your effectiveness in ministry but also your own standing with God. The biblical command to "*make your calling and election sure*" is never more difficult than amid relationship distemper.

Even in the best of times, pastoral ministry demands a high emotional investment, and sometimes you wonder if there's a return. With the addition of conflict, you're tempted to conclude ministry is a total loss.

Not long ago, I sat with Kevin Miller, then LEADERSHIP's *senior associate editor, on a park bench in downtown Denver, and together we listened to a pastor describe his first two years in his congregation. This young pastor was still shaking his head at the anger and accusations that had been directed his way.*

He still didn't understand the significance of it all, but he was beginning to see glimpses of grace, faint movements of God working in himself and the lives of people in the congregation.

Kevin worked with this pastor to disguise the identities but to retell the story. It helps us gain a bit higher ground as we try to get some personal perspective amid the confusion of church conflict.

* * *

The service had ended an hour ago, and Pastor Brian Wells had long since said good-bye to the last departing worshiper, but here he was, still lingering in the cool of the narthex. He didn't know why, really: all he knew is that he felt satisfied.

He'd already sent Carol and the boys home while he closed up, and he knew they'd be impatiently waiting to start Sunday dinner. He leaned forward against the tall panes of glass separating the sanctuary from the narthex and gazed over the empty pews one more time.

The message had been strong that morning. At times his energies had been so focused that he'd seemed to enter what athletes call "the zone," a feeling of effortlessness and euphoria when your concentration is most intense. He was tired now, but it was a good tired, and he wanted to savor it, like a basketball player after a big win.

As he looked across the sanctuary, Brian found it hard to believe he'd been at Community Church of Madison only eight months. He and Carol had fit right in. They'd been asked to dinner more evenings than not. Brian's eyes followed the smooth oak beams up and across the ceiling of the darkened sanctuary, and they seemed like great arms embracing him.

Well, Carol's waiting, he thought, and he started toward the door. He noticed a morning bulletin on the floor near the coat rack. He leaned over and in one smooth swoop picked it up. It wasn't a bulletin after all, he realized as he looked at it, but some sort of leaflet.

RESTORE COMMUNITY CHURCH TO ITS HISTORY OF BIBLICAL INTEGRITY! it said in flaming red. REMOVE PASTOR WELLS!

"Unh." Brian groaned reflexively, as if he'd been punched in the stomach.

"Brian Wells is bent on imposing his liberal views on our church," the leaflet explained. "His utter disregard for the inspiration of Scripture will tear Community Church from its cherished biblical moorings — unless we act now . . ."

Brian scanned down, looking for something identifying who wrote it, but the paper ended with only the words ACT NOW!

He stared at the leaflet. It was his name all right, but he wasn't sure it was talking about him. If anybody was committed to the trustworthiness of Scripture, it was he. He'd even gone to an inerrancy conference last year.

Who would write something like this? His mind quickly filed through people he'd met since coming, but nobody seemed capable of it. *Do a lot of people feel this way, or is it just one or two? Why didn't anyone say something to me?*

Normally, Brian prided himself on his sensitive pastoral antennae. When there was discontent in the congregation, he quickly knew it. But this came without warning. *Why didn't I sense anything?* Brian crumpled the paper in his fist.

When Brian walked into the kitchen at home, everyone stopped eating and looked up. "Your dinner's getting cold," Carol said.

Brian didn't feel like talking, much less eating. He uncrumpled the ball of paper and handed it to her. Carol read the leaflet silently and then looked up with wide eyes. "Brian, who would write that?"

"I don't know, but I'm going to find out," he said, sounding braver than he felt. He walked down the hall into the bedroom and picked up the phone. Then he put it down again. He wasn't sure whom to call. From his predecessor, J. Walter Landis, he had inherited one associate pastor and a youth pastor. They were cordial but still tentative about him. Brian had to admit that was fair; he was tentative about them, too. Still, right now he needed solid support. He finally punched the number for Henry Meyers, chairman of the elder board and a member of the search committee that selected him.

"Henry, have you seen the leaflet about me?" Brian asked.

"What leaflet?"

Brian explained what it said.

"That's crazy," Henry said.

"Henry, who in the world would write something like that?"

"I don't know for sure. But I guess you should know something that happened just before we extended you a call. Landis heard about our intentions and called me long distance from his new church. He said, 'I hear you're going to extend a call to Brian Wells. Let me tell you, Brian's not your man.' "

"But Landis doesn't even know me!"

"No, but he knows you went to Stanton Seminary, and in his mind that brands you. He used to talk against Stanton from the pulpit."

"C'mon. I'm as orthodox as they come."

"I know. I'm just telling you what he used to say."

"How did you respond when he called?" Brian asked.

"I told him, 'Thanks for calling and sharing your opinion, Walter, but the committee feels good about Brian, and we believe he's the person God has led us to call.' That was the end of the conversation. But my guess is some people are against you because of Stanton."

"How many people?"

"Who knows? Probably a handful."

As Brian hung up the telephone, he finally understood why

Landis had preached so often on doctrinal dangers. He must have been utterly devoted to purity. But he'd left the people — some of them, at least — ready to shoot anything that moved.

The next ten days were quiet but unnerving. Brian couldn't shake the feeling he was being watched. Writing his sermon was excruciating. No matter how many times he scrutinized each line, he still feared it could be misinterpreted. In the pulpit he knew he was holding back, yet he felt powerless to do anything about it.

As he shook each hand following the service, he wondered, *Are you for me or against me?* When everyone was gone, he searched the narthex floor for something he hoped he wouldn't, and didn't, find.

The one reprieve was when Larry stopped by his office after the service. Larry's wife was a committed Christian and for years had been trying to persuade her husband to come to church. Larry, an insurance executive, was frank about his distaste for religion, but he had finally consented to try church again. They ended up at Community a month after Brian arrived and had attended regularly ever since.

Larry walked into Brian's office and sat down. He was a big man in his early forties, though he looked older. He leaned forward and looked at Brian. "Pastor," he said, "I want to tell you something. I'm not a Christian yet, but I'm just about there, and it's because of you. You're doing a great job."

When Larry said that, Brian had to smile. *If only you knew how others felt.* But something in the words released the tension.

"Larry, I . . . you don't know how much those words mean to me," Brian managed. "I'm glad you're close to becoming a Christian. You know, there's no time like the present to make that decision, if you're willing."

Brian and Larry talked for fifteen or twenty minutes, and then Larry said he'd made up his mind. He knew it might be hard following Christ, but he was ready to start. They bowed their heads, and Brian led Larry in prayer. When Brian looked up at Larry afterwards, he didn't know which of them was happier. He threw his arms around Larry and gave him a hug even a man his size would remember.

On Friday Brian was sorting through the morning mail and came to a letter with no return address: "Dear Pastor Wells," it began, "You will have to answer to God for your perverted teaching that there is a Mr. and Mrs. God. We can no longer sit back and watch you lead Community Church into error . . ."

Brian quickly read to the bottom: unsigned. Brian read the letter again, but there was no clue, either from the paper or typewriter used, as to who sent it. The line about a "Mr. and Mrs. God" galled and perplexed him. He could understand, perhaps, some people's misconceptions of Stanton Seminary, but this charge was utterly unconnected to reality. It made him sound like a cultist.

Then it hit Brian: *George Mason!* George, a devotional teacher with a national reputation, had spoken at the Wednesday evening service. He had said something like, "We need to be careful in our devotional life that we do not view God as the traditional father, if by that we mean one who is aloof, distant, and uncaring. He's the perfect parent, who also like a loving mother takes a child to his breast." Brian admitted it was a new thought for some people in Community Church, but it certainly squared with Scripture.

The more he thought about the letter, the angrier he became. He hadn't even asked Mason to come; Landis had made all the arrangements before he left! And to construe from what George Mason had said that Brian believed in a Mr. and Mrs. God was absurd. *What am I supposed to do, anyway,* Brian thought, *rip the microphone out of the hands of any guest speaker who has a fresh idea?*

"Cheap shot," Brian muttered under his breath.

Brian had been preaching through the Book of James and had planned to cover James 4:1–12 on Sunday — but now, no way. He'd had enough of being the sitting duck, the passive minister who lets people fire away and keeps on smiling. He might not know who sent the letter or who wrote that leaflet, but they were going to hear about it Sunday, whoever they were. It was time to take a stand.

By three o'clock Brian had an outline and rough draft. The thoughts had flowed. Brian was surprised how productive he could be when he was fired up. Titled "Honor and Honesty," the sermon was going to call to account members of the congregation who had been disregarding both.

Brian was about to head home when the phone rang. It was Vern, an old friend who pastors a large church near Denver. Vern had been through it all during his years of ministry, and even though they didn't see each other often, they made it a habit to check on each other periodically. In fact, Brian had thought about giving him a call a few days earlier.

Brian told Vern about the leaflet and the unsigned letter. "But this Sunday I'm going to set things straight," Brian said. "I can't let this kind of thing keep happening."

"I can appreciate how you feel," Vern said. "But I'd think twice before I blasted anybody from the pulpit. When I was an associate at Third Street, Sawyer started being attacked by people, and he took the battle into the pulpit. All that did was make people defensive and angry. The people who hadn't done anything wrong felt, *Hey, I like him. What's he after me for?*"

"So what am I supposed to do?" Brian asked. "Just let these people continue their guerrilla warfare?"

"Truth will triumph. Where you're wrong, admit it. Where they're wrong, don't defend yourself. But just focus on what God has for you to say. As hard as it is, don't take your fighting into the pulpit — truth will win out."

Brian lay awake in bed that night. The leaflet and letter hurt so much he didn't want to think about them, but he couldn't stop. They were so unfair, so one-sided, so insane. But Vern was usually right. If he dropped the bomb on Sunday, he'd wound not only the guilty but also countless innocents. Part of the passage in James he'd studied began to come back to him: "Humble yourselves before the Lord, and he will lift you up." Then Brian drifted asleep.

When Brian walked into the pulpit Sunday, he slipped out of his pocket a card on which he'd handlettered TRUTH WILL TRIUMPH. He laid it in front of him and took a deep breath. He'd never been angry and afraid and calm all at once. But somehow he was. He launched into, ironically, James 4:1 — "What causes fights and quarrels among you?" — and when he finished preaching eleven verses later, he walked back to his seat with his head up. He'd had the chance to lash out, but he hadn't used it.

After the service, Henry Meyers pulled him aside. "Pastor, I think we've found our man."

"I got a call late last night from Ed Anderson," Henry continued. "He said that under your teaching, Community Church was falling into error and that we as elders were responsible to do something about it."

"What did you say?"

"I said yes, that was our responsibility and asked him what sort of problems he was having with your teaching. He said that you did not believe in the inerrancy of the Bible and as a result had fallen into deception, including that there is a Mr. and Mrs. God."

Henry stopped and looked at Brian, and Brian nodded for him to keep going.

" 'Well, Ed, to be honest,' I said, 'the other elders doubt very seriously whether he believes there's some sort of husband-and-wife God.' "

Brian was encouraged by the support.

"Then he got really mad," Henry continued. "He said he wasn't the only one who felt this way, that a lot of other people were also concerned, and that if we didn't care about the Bible, they'd find a pastor and elders who did."

"What did you say?"

"At that point, I knew we had to give him a chance to air his grievances. I asked him if he'd be willing to talk to the elders about his concerns, with you present to defend yourself."

"Did he take you up on it?"

"We set a meeting for this Saturday, provided you and all the elders can make it."

On Saturday morning, Brian was in the church lounge at 8:30.

The meeting wasn't scheduled until 9:00, but he wanted to pick a chair he'd be comfortable in and also to pray for a few moments. He had bags under his eyes from a sleepless night. Every time he had awakened, though, he thought through what he could say to defend himself; so he was feeling confident about the meeting.

Brian didn't know much about Ed except what Henry had told him: in his fifties, a fairly wealthy attorney, and a natural leader used to running his own show. He had wanted to be on the board, but Landis had twice nixed the idea, and he was probably still smarting from that.

When Ed arrived, shortly after nine, he chose a chair directly across the room from Brian. He grunted a "Good morning" to everyone so far gathered and sat in silence.

When the last elder arrived, Henry wasted no time beginning the meeting. "Ed, we're here to listen to whatever you have to say to us. We've asked Brian to be here to answer questions that come up and to clarify what he believes and teaches. So why don't you start."

Ed glanced down at a legal pad in his lap and then looked across at Brian.

"Pastor," he said, "how many epistles are there in the New Testament?"

Brian panicked. He didn't know what Ed was driving at, and he wasn't prepared for that question. "I don't know the exact number offhand," Brian said, "but let's see . . . there's Romans, two to the Corinthians . . ."

Brian's mind went blank. He couldn't even think of the next book in the New Testament. "Uh, I don't know, but I'd say about twenty or so."

"Twenty-one," Ed informed him. "What I want to know," he said, looking around at the elders, "is why you wrote in the last church newsletter that there were twenty-eight."

"I, uh . . ." Brian stalled, and then it came to him. "I said in that article I was also counting the letters to the seven churches in the Book of Revelation. Besides, the point of the article was not the exact number but that each of us is an epistle, known and read by all. People read our actions to see if our faith means anything."

"That's a nice, allegorical way to avoid the fact that you don't know the Bible very well."

"Regardless," Henry broke in, "that's a minor issue. Let's get to the heart of the matter."

"All right," Ed said. "You don't believe the Bible is inerrant, do you?" He leaned forward and looked at Brian.

"That's not true. I believe the Scriptures are without error."

"But you never preach on it."

"Well, not all the time, but since I've been here I've preached one sermon on the reliability of Scripture, and all my sermons show the Bible as our sole authority."

"But would you be willing to sign a public statement saying that you believe in inerrancy?"

"I already have. When I accepted the call to Community Church, I signed a statement saying I was in complete agreement with the church's constitution and statement of faith, and that includes inerrancy."

Gordon, one of the elders, joined the attack. "You went to Stanton Seminary. Would you say they teach inerrancy?"

Brian was stunned that Gordon was supporting Ed's cause. "I can't vouch for all the professors there, but I know I believe in inerrancy."

"Gentleman," Ed said, looking away from Brian, "what you have here is a man who says he believes in inerrancy, who will even sign a statement saying he believes it, but who in his heart of hearts really doesn't believe it. How can a man like that be our pastor?"

Brian didn't know whether to laugh or cry. Was he supposed to sign in blood?

The rest of the meeting was a stalemate. Ed refused to accept Brian's professions of belief. Henry finally tried to close the meeting. "Ed, thank you for being willing to share your concerns with us. I don't know what to say. Pastor Brian says he believes in inerrancy and has even signed a statement to that effect. To us, that's enough proof. If it's not to you, we're sorry."

"You mean you're not going to take a vote?" Ed demanded.

"A vote on what?"

"A vote on whether we ought to remove this man as our pastor."

"I don't see why that's necessary, but yes, if you want us to go on record, we can take a vote. All those in favor of removing Brian Wells as pastor of Community Church, say 'aye.' "

"Aye," said Gordon loudly — with Ed, who couldn't even vote.

"All those opposed?"

"Nay," said the rest of the room.

"I want to warn you," said Ed as he stood up. "Gordon and I aren't the only ones who are concerned about the pastor. His own staff doesn't support him. I love this church. It kills me to leave it. But if you men are too weak to remove a pastor who's subverting it, we'll find a church that does preach the Word." Then he left, with Gordon close behind.

As Brian drove home, he felt sick. What had Ed meant by "his own staff doesn't support him"? Was that another one of his outrageous claims, or was there some truth to it? And how did Ed know? Had he and the staff been meeting behind Brian's back? It hurt, too, that Gordon, who ought to know better, had turned against him. He'd been so supportive on the elder retreat, and now in the middle of a meeting, he decides he can't trust his own pastor.

Brian was proud of the rest of the elders, though. They'd been pure gold, tested and refined. They and Brian had "won," though strangely, Brian almost didn't care. Maybe that's what bothered him most about this whole thing. No matter how wrong Ed and Gordon might be, the whole affair had inflicted such a severe emotional beating that Brian hadn't felt good for anything. *What kind of ministry can you have when you're constantly under siege?* he wondered.

Three weeks later Brian found out that Ed and Gordon and about seventy-five other people had started meeting on the other side of town. He called Henry Meyers to let him know.

"So they carried through on their threat," Henry said.

"Yeah. They're renting the Seventh-day Adventist church building on Sunday mornings, and they're talking about calling a pastor soon."

"There's not much we can do about Ed, but it sure hurts to see so many people go with him."

"It hurts me, too," Brian said, "but in a way I'm almost relieved. Maybe this is natural fallout when a new pastor comes. Maybe now things will calm down and we can get back to ministry."

"Brian, I hate to tell you this since you just said that, but remember in our meeting with Ed, how he said even the staff doesn't support you? I've been puzzling over that statement ever since."

"Me, too," Brian said. "I couldn't tell whether he was bluffing or whether he knew something we didn't. And I couldn't exactly confront Doug and Tim: 'Are you loyal to me? Have you been meeting with Ed?' "

"Well, my wife was talking with Tim's wife, and she said that the month before that leaflet came out, Ed invited Tim and Doug over to his house. He wanted to know what they thought about how things were going in the church. Apparently Tim supported you, but Doug was pretty negative. It upset Tim and his wife, but they didn't feel right saying anything about it earlier."

Brian hung up, leaned back in his chair, and looked at the ceiling. *So it's not over*, he thought. Now the problem rumbled within his staff. But what could he do, fire a person because he criticized him? During his own days as an associate, he hadn't always agreed with his senior pastor. Still, this was different, and Brian didn't know what to do.

Several Sundays later, just before his sermon, Brian looked out and saw Larry sitting near the back. Suddenly all the anger and frustration he had felt over the past months came bubbling up. *Here's this new believer*, he thought, *looking for a warm and safe place to*

*grow in Christ, and we can't give it to him. My faith is hardly strong enough
to stand all this backbiting and gossip, and we're subjecting him to it. He's
never going to make it.*

Complicating the whole matter was that Larry and Doug lived
near each other, and their kids had become good friends. Brian
wasn't sure how close they were, but if Doug were making comments critical of him or the church, Larry would probably hear
them. And if Brian and Doug had to part ways, Larry would witness
the whole mess. Brian didn't know if Larry's tender faith could
withstand any more church dissension.

In the spring, Brian asked Christian scholar and writer R. T.
Bradfield to speak at Community Church. Following the church's
usual policy, he had his secretary send Bradfield a copy of the
church's doctrinal statement to sign. Bradfield called him the next
week and said he deeply wanted to come to Community, but
couldn't in good conscience endorse some of the fine points of
eschatology that were part of the statement.

Brian said he didn't think that would pose any problem, but
he wanted to get the board's approval. He was still tender from the
blow-up over George Mason's comments.

At the elder board meeting the following Thursday, Brian
explained what Bradfield had said.

"I've read two of Bradfield's books," said Henry. "Heavy
stuff, but good! And didn't he write the book on biblical inerrancy?
To refuse to allow him to speak because of a minor point of eschatology is ridiculous."

The other elders agreed wholeheartedly. "Of course, we're
going to have him," said one. "Besides, nothing in the constitution
says a speaker has to sign the statement or he can't preach."

Brian thought Doug looked disgruntled. But he wasn't sure.

At the next weekly staff meeting, Brian was going over the
preaching and worship calendar for the coming quarter.

"How's it look to you?" Brian asked Doug.

"I've been meaning to say something about this, and now seems like the time," said Doug. "A lot of people have said to me, 'We need more meat, more depth in our messages.' So I was thinking it might be good if you preached on Sunday morning and let me feed the people on Sunday nights."

Brian consciously tried to keep his expression steady. He could handle criticism, but if "more meat" meant a preaching style like Doug's, he had grave reservations. One time Doug was preaching and asked all the men in the congregation to stand. Then he said, "Women, look at these men. If one-third of these men became as spiritual as they ought to be, this church would be a different place." He was a master of intimidation.

"Let me think about that for a while, Doug," Brian said. He wanted to make sure he handled this right, and he was afraid if they got into it now, the quiet exchange might escalate into verbal war.

The following week Brian decided on his strategy. He was going to be on a badly needed vacation the following month, so he asked Doug to take the Sunday evening service while he was gone, and at least one Sunday night each month from then on. As much as Brian disagreed with some of Doug's preaching tactics, he wanted to support him; Doug was a capable discipleship leader and had given six years to Community Church.

When he presented the idea, Doug seemed happy for the opportunities, and that helped blunt the news that Brian didn't think it was time for him to take every Sunday evening just yet.

On the first Sunday evening of their trip, Brian and Carol stayed in a Holiday Inn outside Indianapolis. Brian was sitting up in bed reading *USA Today* when the phone rang. *Who could be calling me?* he wondered as he walked over to the phone. *No one knows I'm here.*

"Pastor, I'm really sorry to bother you, especially so late." It was Henry Meyers.

"Henry! What's going on?"

"It's Doug. You know he preached tonight."

"Yes?"

"Brian, he really blasted the elders. He said we were weak, not being completely truthful with the congregation. And since we didn't measure up to the biblical standards, we shouldn't be followed until we return to complete truthfulness."

"Oh no."

"I feel bad calling you like this, but the congregation is in an uproar. I've had five phone calls about it in the last hour. I hate to suggest this, but I think if you could be here, you could calm things down."

The next morning, Brian headed their Reliant wagon north on I-65 back toward Madison. Carol sat in silence, and the kids, knowing something was wrong, were subdued. Brian didn't know what to say to Carol. She understood — she really did — but he felt like Scrooge tearing her away from this vacation. She'd been waiting for it for months, and all the promises that they'd get away again soon sounded cheap.

As they drove past the fields of knee-high corn, Brian formulated what he would say to Doug. And every now and then his thoughts would wander to Larry. *I was afraid this was going to happen,* he thought. *How's he supposed to understand that Christ is great and it's just us Christians that are the problem? Larry, friend, if you give it all up, you have no one to blame but us.*

That evening, Brian and the elders met with Doug in an emergency meeting.

"Doug, you have publicly charged the elders of this church with not being truthful," Brian began. "That's a serious charge. Explain what you mean."

"I've been in this church for six years," he said, "and I've always been able to support and work with its leaders. But it deeply disturbs me when I see elders who don't have integrity on fiscal matters and who hide the fact they let any speaker, no matter how off-base, into the pulpit."

"Which speakers, for example?"

"R. T. Bradfield. And anyone who can't sign this church's

statement of faith ought not to be allowed to speak in its pulpit."

"We discussed that at the elders' meeting," Henry snapped. "If you had a problem with it, why didn't you say something then, rather than immaturely blasting us in a public worship service? There's nothing wrong with Bradfield, anyway. He's as orthodox as anyone here."

The meeting lasted over an hour. Doug never did produce any evidence of financial wrongdoing — Brian knew he couldn't because there wasn't any. The issue at heart was Doug's objection to the church's "weak leadership."

Near the end, Doug said, "I'm stunned. Community Church has been my home, my family. But since it's clear that you men are not willing to lead this church in a godly direction, I can no longer be part of it. I resign."

Brian hurt inside, but he didn't try to stop Doug. In truth, he didn't know any other way to resolve the problem. How do you answer a charge that you aren't godly?

"Doug," Henry said, "we accept your resignation, though we want you to know we're sorry you feel this way. And I personally want to ask your forgiveness for snapping at you earlier in this meeting. Please forgive me."

The room was silent. Then Doug nodded at Henry, stood, and walked out.

On Sunday the church held a farewell reception of sorts for Doug following the service. Brian saw Larry say good-bye to Doug. Larry's kids were crying. Larry had to know all the dirt behind the resignation. Brian wanted to run over and say something to him, but what could he say?

For five weeks Brian didn't hear anything about Doug. Then the leader of an adult Sunday school class told Brian half his class had stopped coming; they were meeting with Doug on Sunday mornings now. When Brian checked into it, he found that in the two weeks since Doug's group had met, attendance had swelled to over one hundred.

The news sent Brian into an emotional tailspin. When Ed and

all his people left, he'd almost felt relieved, but to have the same thing happen again so soon was too much. *I must be setting some sort of ecclesiastical record*, Brian thought. He could imagine the headlines in the Stanton alumni magazine: WELLS' CHURCH HAS RECORD SECOND SPLIT IN HIS FIRST TWO YEARS.

What am I doing wrong? Brian thought, spinning a pencil in circles on his desk. *Oh, God, I'm tired.*

Brian looked down at his desk calendar, hoping his afternoon would magically be open, but two appointments stared at him. The first was with Larry. His secretary must have set it up.

That's the crowning blow, he thought. *Larry's going to come in here and say, "Pastor Wells, I've given this Christianity thing a fair shake, but it's just not all it's cracked up to be."*

Larry came five minutes late, and when he walked in, Brian thought he looked troubled. He sat down in the brown chair across from Brian's desk, then leaned forward. Brian braced himself.

"Pastor," he said, "this last year has been hell for me."

"That sounds rough. Tell me about it," Brian said mechanically.

"My boss is the most abrasive person I've ever known," he said. "He never has a kind word about anyone or anything. For three years I've sweated under that, and then I came to Community Church — "

And you found we Christians aren't any better, Brian mentally completed his sentence.

"And I watched you," Larry went on. "I watched the slander, the accusations, all the guff. You had every right to retaliate. And you didn't."

Brian was silent.

"I figured if God could help you not to retaliate, with all you went through, then he could help me not to retaliate with what I went through. So I went back to my boss, and I did something I've never done before in my life — it had to be God, because I couldn't do it — I apologized to my boss, and I asked his forgiveness for the way I've bucked him and for the bad attitudes I've had."

Brian opened his mouth to say something, but he couldn't get anything out.

"So that's why I came in here today. I wanted you to know that in the last year you not only helped me meet the Lord, you also proved to me that, in the middle of hard times, God is real."

Brian's eyes started to well with tears.

"If you didn't come to Madison for anybody else, Pastor, you came for me."

Brian started to cry. He knew he must have looked like a fool in front of Larry, but he didn't care. He let the tears come.

— *Kevin Miller*

*The people of God won't become "the church triumphant"
without first being "the church militant," and I mean
militant.*

— *Mark Galli*

Epilogue

A church without conflict is not merely unimaginable, it also seems to be outside of God's design, for the people of God won't become "the church triumphant" without first being "the church militant," and I mean *militant*.

People in congregations are constantly militating for one thing or another. Sometimes it's about things seemingly inconsequential — clapping in worship. Other times, it gets immediately to substantive issues: more money for missions, whether divorced people should serve in leadership.

In any case, it's in the middle of the militant that we are called to find strategies for turning mere battles into redeeming encounters. Because no matter the issue, it's *people* who are in conflict. And although we're trying to "manage conflict" and "work through issues," we are primarily learning to get along with people, more particularly, our brothers and sisters in Christ.

In this book, our authors have shown us some practical steps for living together in truth, forgiveness, and grace, things for which by God's design, we are called to militate.

And when we learn how so to live, when in the midst of anger (some of it righteous) and dissension (some of it called for), we manage to love our neighbor in the pew, we are readying ourselves for life in the church triumphant.

William Penn, the famous Quaker, put it bluntly: "No pain, no palm; no thorns, no throne; no gall, no glory; no cross, no crown."

He might have added, "No conflict, no church."

www.ingramcontent.com/pod-product-compliance
Ingram Content Group UK Ltd.
Pitfield, Milton Keynes, MK11 3LW, UK
UKHW020812120325
456141UK00001B/69